TRANSACTIONS

of the

American Philosophical Society

Held at Philadelphia for Promoting Useful Knowledge

VOLUME 81, Part 4

Candidates Defeated in Roman Elections: Some Ancient Roman "Also-Rans"

T. ROBERT S. BROUGHTON

Professor Emeritus of Classics, University of North Carolina

AMERICAN PHILOSOPHICAL SOCIETY

Independence Square Philadelphia

1991

Library of Congress Catalog
Card Number 90-56339
International Standard Book Number 0–87169–814–5
US ISSN 0065–9746

CONTENTS

ABBREVIATIONS

ANRW	*Aufstieg und Niedergang der römischen Welt*
Briscoe, *Comm.* 1	J. Briscoe, *A Commentary on Livy*, Books xxxi–xxxiii
Briscoe, *Comm.* 2	J. Briscoe, *A Commentary on Livy*, Books xxxiv–xxxvii
Denniston, *Commentary*	J. D. Denniston, M. Tulli Ciceronis in M. Antonium Orationes Philippicae Prima et Secunda, with Introduction, Notes and Appendices
MRR	T. R. S. Broughton, *The Magistrates of the Roman Republic*
Marshall, *Asconius*	B. A. Marshall, *A Historical Commentary on Asconius*
Mommsen, *StR*	Th. Mommsen, *Römisches Staatsrecht*
Münzer, *APF*	Fr. Münzer, *Römische Adelsparteien und Adelsfamilien*
RE	*Realencyclopädie der Classischen Altertumswissenschaft*
Rilinger, *Einfluss*	R. Rilinger, *Der Einfluss des Wahlleiters bei den römischen Konsulwahlen von 366 bis 50 v. Chr.*
SB, *CLA*	D. R. Shackleton Bailey, *Cicero's Letters to Atticus*
SB, *CLF*	D. R. Shackleton Bailey, Cicero, *Epistulae ad Familiares*
SB, *CLQF*	D. R. Shackleton Bailey, Cicero, *Epistulae ad Quintum Fratrem et ad M. Brutum*
SB, *Two Studies*	D. R. Shackleton Bailey, *Two Studies in Roman Nomenclature*
SB, *Onomasticon*	D. R. Shackleton Bailey, *Onomasticon to Cicero's Speeches*
Sumner, *Orators*	G. V. Sumner, *The Orators in Cicero's Brutus: Prosopography and Chronology*
Suolahti, *RC*	Jaakko Suolahti, *The Roman Censors. A Study in Social Structure*
L. R. Taylor, *RVA*	L. R. Taylor, *Roman Voting Assemblies from the Hannibalic War to the Dictatorship of Caesar*
Wiseman, *New Men*	T. P. Wiseman, *New Men in the Roman Senate, B.C. 139 and A.D. 14*

I. INTRODUCTION*

It is the purpose of this work to collect and present in context the names of members of a somewhat neglected group, the candidates in Roman elections for magistracies and priesthoods in the Middle and Late Republic who competed unsuccessfully. In the listing of these candidates for the major magistracies, the consulship, the praetorship, and the aedileships, I have arranged those for each magistracy in two groups. The first consists of the candidates who competed throughout until the votes were counted and the victors announced, candidates who had suffered defeat (*repulsa*) in the full sense of the word. The second group, less certain and more vaguely definable, consists of those who began to compete and either withdrew or were prevented from proceeding further. Some, who merely began to canvass for support, or whose application for candidacy (*ratio*) was not accepted by the presiding magistrate, were technically not candidates at all, but they should still be considered in relation to the competition. Although examples may be cited from other periods, the period that is chiefly considered runs from 218 B.C., the beginning of the Second Punic War, to 44 B.C., the assassination of Julius Caesar, the period for which the sources, among which Livy and Cicero are the most important, provide more details about candidates for elective office.

Like ourselves, the Romans of the Republic were much more interested in recording the achievements and preserving the memory of the victorious candidates. Relatively few of the names of defeated candidates have been preserved, even in years when there appears to have been no lack of competition. Some have won a place in the record through involvement in interesting incidents and others because they appear in personal anecdotes. A high percentage of the defeated candidates for the consulship are recorded because they competed in a time of crisis, as in 216, or in an election of special interest, as in 189, and

*Thanks are due to friends and colleagues for their interest and help, and particularly to Professor Jerzy Linderski, who read the manuscript, saved me from errors, and called my attention to the regular membership of many defeated candidates in the Roman senate. What faults and errors remain are attributable to me alone.

many more of them (over half) because they persisted until they were successful, and often they had distinguished later careers.

The known names are listed alphabetically, with citation of sources, under each of the magistracies in order—first the consulship, then the censorship, then in succession, the praetorship, the aedileships, the tribunate of the plebs, the quaestorship, and the one lone example of defeat for the military tribunate; and, finally, the defeated candidates for the major priestly colleges, with inclusion of the pontifex maximus, elections for all of which were held under special conditions. For the first three, the consuls, censors, and praetors, the elections were held in the *Comitia Centuriata*, with a consul or an interrex as presiding magistrate; for the curule aediles, the quaestors, and other minor magistracies, they were held in the *Comitia Tributa*, with a consul or a praetor in charge, but the tribunes and the aediles of the plebs were elected in the *Concilium Plebis* with a tribune as presiding officer. In the times when the laws required elections to membership in the priestly colleges, they were held in a special tribal assembly of 17 tribes, chosen by lot from the total number of thirty-five, with a consul in charge.[1] Only the elections for the consulship provide a considerable number of examples of defeated candidates, and these constitute a very small proportion of the probable number who were defeated in the elections throughout the years.

Lack of evidence makes it hazardous to attempt even an approximate estimate of the number of the defeated consular candidates between 218 and 44 B.C. The total number of candidates in any one year is known only for four elections, those for 216, 192, 184, and 63. In 216, according to Livy (22.34–35), there were six, three patricians for the one available patrician place, and three plebeians; the addition of L. Aemilius Paullus brings the total to seven. For 192, there were seven (Liv. 35.10.2–3), three patricians and four plebeians. For 184, Livy (39.13.2) lists four patricians and three plebeians, seven in all, six of whom had been defeated before. For 63, the year of Cicero's consulship, Asconius (82C) lists seven candidates, two patricians and five plebeians. For 192 and 189, Livy (35.24.4; 37.47.7) names the three patricians in each year who were rivals for the single available place, and the one plebeian who was successful, M'. Acilius Glabrio for 191, and M. Fulvius Nobilior for 189. As

---

[1]Mommsen, *StR* 2³, 27–34; cf. 1³, 469, note 2; cf. *MRR* 3.11–12, on Scaurus (140), and 82–83, on Domitius (21). On the time of election to priestly colleges, see Cic. *Ad Brut.* 1.5.3, and Shackleton Bailey's comment *CLQF, ad loc.* 233–234; J. Linderski, *HSPh* 76 (1972) 181–200, esp. 191–193. On the election of the pontifex maximus, see L. R. Taylor, *CPh* 37 (1942) 421–424.

Briscoe[2] points out in the case of Glabrio, it is quite unlikely that either of them was elected unopposed. This information is clearly an insufficient base for a numerical estimate, but it may be worth noting that if there were an average of three defeated candidates for the consulship, a number less than the four or five in the examples cited above, in each year from 218 to 44, the total would be 522, more than 12 times the total of known defeated candidates listed below.

If such a situation is even approximately correct, one can assume, especially with the development of the *Leges Annales* and a regular *Cursus honorum*, that with very rare exceptions (such as Pompey), candidates for the major magistracies were already senators. The facts that there were only two consulships each year, with only occasional opportunity for a suffect, and that praetorships were not numerous (two from 242 to 227, four to 197, and in effect six until Sulla raised the number to eight), when considered with the probable number of candidates in each election, suggest that at almost all times the Senate included a considerable number of defeated candidates. It is probable that in a body, once of three hundred and later of six hundred members, many in the lower positions would have neither the means nor the desire to compete for the higher magistracies, but among those who competed only a few could be elected, and many even among those who could count on status, means, and support were likely still to fail in the contest for the praetorship and the consulship. One cannot do more than speculate on the effect of this, but given that election depended largely on personal connections, status, and support, and less on programs for legislation or reform, the general trend, in spite of personal rivalries, resentments, and enmities, would probably tend to be conservative and assimilative. Attacks on senatorial authority were disruptive.

In the record of many of the candidates for the consulship listed below defeat was only a temporary setback. Many persisted and attained the consulship in a later year, and some, as for example, M. Aemilius Lepidus (No. 2, below) or L. Aemilius Paullus (No. 4, below), achieved careers of great distinction. Of the 41 candidates listed in Chapter II, Part 1, below, 24 won the consulship by repeated attempts. Two of them, P. Rutilius Rufus (No. 32) and Ser. Sulpicius Rufus (No. 37) attained it only after ten years for the former and eleven for the latter, though with little apparent effort on their part. On the whole, there is a high proportion of later victors.

---

[2] J. Briscoe, *Comm.2, on Livy, Books xxxiv-xxxvii*, p. 180, on Liv. 35.24.4–5.

Several passages in Livy suggest that a defeat, at least of candidates of noble family, might favor rather than prejudice success in a later attempt. The later success of Scipio Nasica (No. 14) is reported with the comment: "*Ut dilatum viro tali, non negatum, honorem appareret, consulatus datus est*" (Liv. 35.24.5). In the hotly contested election for the consulship of 184, the three patrician candidates are described as "*veteres candidatos et ab repulsis eo magis debitum, quia primo negatus est, honorem repetentes*" (Liv. 39.25.6), and the attitude of the plebeian candidates is similarly expressed, "*et hi repulsis in spem impetrandi tandem aliquando honoris dilati.*" We are not told if this aroused some extra resentment when P. Claudius, with the help of active canvassing by his brother, who was a consul in office at the time, won the patrician place on his first attempt.

As I noted above, it is a generally, and rightly, accepted view that the success of candidates for office in Roman elections depended largely upon their personal status and connections, and the support and favor they could secure by personal contacts and by canvassing the voters, and that it depended much less, except in extreme cases, or in a time of crisis, on statements of policy or a legislative program.[3] For what it may be worth, a consideration of the defeated candidates makes its small contribution in support and confirmation of this view of the importance of personal factors. But some room should be left, as Cicero's remarks in the *Pro Murena* and the *Pro Plancio* emphasize, for the volatility of the voters and the changeable nature of popular favor.[4]

---

[3]Note the emphasis on personal factors and connections in Cic. *Att.* 1.1, and additional emphasis on personal canvassing in the *Commentariolum Petitionis*. On the point that the major part of Roman legislation was carried in the form of *plebiscita* by tribunes in the *Concilium Plebis*, see L. R. Taylor, *RVA* 6–7, 16–17, 60–61.

[4]Cic. *Mur.* 36: *nihil est incertius volgo, nihil obscurius voluntate hominum, nihil fallacius ratione tota comitiorum; Planc.* 8; *nunc tantum disputo de iure populi, qui et potest et solet non numquam dignos praeterire; nec, si a populo praeteritus est quem non oportuit, a iudicibus condemnandus est qui praeteritus non est.*

II. CANDIDATES FOR THE CONSULSHIP

1. Candidates Defeated in Elections

1. *M'. Acilius Glabrio* (35) Pr. 196

A candidate for the consulship of 192, Glabrio competed with three patricians, P. Cornelius Scipio Nasica (350; see below, No. 14), Cn. Manlius Vulso (91; see below, No. 25), and L. Quinctius Flamininus (43), and three plebeians, Cn. Domitius Ahenobarbus (18), C. Laelius (2; see below, No. 18), and C. Livius Salinator (29; see below, No. 21).[1] L. Flamininus and Cn. Domitius were elected. The next year Glabrio, most probably with the support of the Scipios, was elected to the consulship of 191 (*MRR* 1.352).

2. *M. Aemilius Lepidus* (68) Pr. 191

Lepidus was a candidate for the consulship of 189, who was criticized at that time for leaving his province, Sicily, without first securing permission from the Senate, in order to compete (Liv. 37.47.6). His competitors for the one possible patrician place were Cn. Manlius Vulso (91; see below, No. 25) and M. Valerius Messalla (252; see below, No. 41), and the plebeian M. Fulvius Nobilior (91). Fulvius was elected alone, as none of the others had received a majority of the votes of the centuries. According to Livy's account, Fulvius took office at once, and on the next day presided over the election of his colleague. Casting Lepidus down, he announced the election of Manlius.[2] Messalla had received little or no support (*iacuit*).

---

[1] Liv. 35.10.3 and 24.4–5; cf. Briscoe, *Comm.* 1, p. 164, and *Comm.* 2, pp. 158–159, and 180; *MRR* 1.350–352.

[2] Liv. 37.47.7: *Fulvius consul unus creatur, cum ceteri centurias non explessent, isque postero die Cn. Manlium, Lepido deiecto,—nam Messalla iacuit—collegam dixit.* Livy makes no mention of an *interregnum*, but a procedure that allowed Fulvius to take office immediately and preside over the election of his colleague suggests strongly that there was one (see Mommsen, *StR* 1³, 217, n. 4, and Rilinger, *Einfluss* 18 n. 42). Briscoe's suggestion (*Comm.* 2, p. 365) that the election took place on Pr. Id. Mart., at that time the last day of the consular year, and that Fulvius took office and held the election for his colleague the next day takes no account that in the Roman calendar there were no comitial days from March 13 to 17 (cf. A. K. Michels, *The Calendar of the Roman Republic*). Briscoe also sug-

Near the end of the consular year 189, Lepidus, this time a candidate for the consulship of 188, was again defeated in an election over which his enemy, Fulvius, presided as consul, and cast him down again.[3] Livy reports no names of other candidates besides those of the victors, M. Valerius Messalla (252) and C. Livius Salinator (29), who had both been defeated the previous year. Lepidus was finally elected to the consulship of 187 (MRR 1.367), and later became famous for his brilliant career as consul for a second time, censor, pontifex maximus, and princeps senatus (see MRR, Index, 2.526).

3. Mam. Aemilius Lepidus Livianus (60) Pr. by 81

According to Cicero,[4] the stinginess of Mamercus in bypassing, although he was wealthy, the aedileship with its expensive burden of public games and entertainments, led to his defeat when he competed for the consulship. His previous associations with Sulla led Badian and Sumner[5] to identify him as the candidate for the consulship of 78 whom Sulla favored over the M. Aemilius Lepidus (72) who was elected with Pompey's support (MRR 2.116). A fragment from Sallust's Histories[6] suggests that the Mamercus in whose favor the elder C. Scribonius Curio (10) was asked to withdraw from the competition for the consulship of 77 had previously submitted himself to the votes of the people. With this aid, Mamercus was elected for 77. On Curio, see below, Chapter II, Part 2, No. 23.

4. L. Aemilius Paullus (114) Pr. 191

Aemilius Paullus, when a candidate for the consulship of 184, was one of a group of three patricians whom Livy de-

---

gests that Livy was perhaps mistaken either in using the words *postero die* or in the name of the presiding magistrate; but note Lepidus' remark in Liv. 40.46.14: *bis a M. Fulvio se certo consulatu deiectum.*

[3]Liv. 38.35.1: *cum M. Aemilium Lepidum inimicum eo quoque anno petentem deiecisset.* On the ways the presiding magistrate could influence the result of the elections, see L. R. Taylor, *RVA,* 104–105; Rilinger, *Einfluss,* 120–121 and 146–147. The accounts of Lepidus' defeats serve as a background for his success in attaining the consulship of 187 in his third candidacy (Liv. 38.42.1), and for his resounding public reconciliation with Fulvius when they were elected as colleagues in the censorship in 179 (Liv. 40.45.7–46.16; MRR 1.392).

[4]*Off.* 2.58: *vitanda tamen suspicio est avaritiae. Mamerco, homini divitissimo, praetermissio aedilitatis consulatus repulsam attulit.*

[5]Badian, *Studies,* 234, note 17; Sumner, "Manius or Mamercus?" *JRS* 54 (1964) 41–46. Note the doubts of N. Criniti, M. Aemilius Q.f. M.n. Lepidus, "Ut Ignis in Stipula," *MIL* 30 (1969) Fasc. 4, 364–366, esp. note 136. See also Marshall, *Asconius,* 227, 255.

[6]Fr. 1.86M: *Curionem quaesit, uti adulescentior et a populo suffragiis integer aetati concederet Mamerci.*

scribes as *veteres candidatos*.[7] He must therefore have competed in some previous year, or even, as Valerius Maximus vaguely suggests (7.5.3: *aliquotiens frustra consulatum petiit*), had done so more than once. This candidacy must be dated after his return early in 187 from Asia Minor, where he was one of a senatorial committee of ten legates who assisted Manlius Vulso in the settlement after the defeat of Antiochus the Great (*MRR* 363, 367).

For the consulship of 184, Paullus competed for the one available patrician place with Q. Fabius Labeo (91; see below, No. 16) and Ser. Sulpicius Galba (57; see below, No. 35), both of whom were, like himself, *veteres candidati*, and P. Claudius Pulcher (305), whose brother, the consul then in office, campaigned actively on his behalf and secured his election. The three plebeian candidates (*gratiosi homines*)[8] were Q. Terentius Culleo (43; see below, No. 37), Cn. Baebius Tanphilus (44; see below, No. 7), and L. Porcius Licinus (25), who was elected along with P. Claudius (*MRR* 1.372).

5. *M. Aemilius Scaurus* (140) Pr. by 119

Scaurus, when a candidate for the consulship of 116, was defeated, surprisingly, as Cicero remarks,[9] by Q. Fabius Maximus Eburnus (211). He was elected the next year to the consulship of 115. He was censor in 109, and princeps senatus from 115 until his death in 89 or 88 (*MRR* 1.532; 2.44).

6. *L. Aurelius Cotta* (102) Pr. 70

Cotta, and L. Manlius Torquatus (79), when they were candidates in 66 for the consulships of 65, were defeated in the regular election by P. Cornelius Sulla (386) and P. Autronius Paetus (7). The victors were in turn accused of *ambitus* under the Lex Calpurnia of 67, P. Sulla by the younger L. Manlius, son of the defeated candidate, and upon conviction were debarred from office (Cic. *Sulla* 11, 49–50, 81; *Fin.*

---

[7]Liv. 39.32.5: *veteres candidatos et ab repulsis eo magis debitum, quia primo negatus est, honorem repententes.*

[8]Liv. 39.32.8: *gratiosi homines . . . et hi repulsis in spem impetrandi tandem aliquando honoris dilati.*

[9]*Quis Scaurum, hominem gravissimum, civem egregium, fortissimum senatorem a Q. Maximo superari posse arbitratus est?* (*Mur* 36). In this passage Cicero refers to several examples of the unpredictability of voters in consular elections. On Scaurus, see also G. M. Bloch, *M. Aemilius Scaurus*, 13–14; R. L. Bates, *Proc. Amer. Philos. Soc.* 130 (1986) 251–288, esp. 255–256.

2.62; Ascon. 88 C; cf. *MRR* 2.157).[10] Cotta and Torquatus were successful in the supplementary election (*MRR* 2.157).

7. *Cn. Baebius Tamphilus* (41) Pr. 199

A candidate for the consulship of 184, Baebius competed with four patricians and two plebeians (Liv. 39.32.8; see above, on L. Aemilius Paullus [114], No. 4), when P. Claudius Pulcher (305) and L. Porcius Licinus (25) were elected. Livy's statement (39.32.8: *et hi repulsis in spem tandem aliquando impetrandi honoris dilati*) reveals that Baebius and the other plebeians had been defeated candidates before. Baebius was elected consul for 182 (Liv. 39.56.4; *MRR* 1.381–382).

7a. *? C. Billienus* (Bellienus 4, cf. 3) Pr. ca. 107

C. Billienus was a praetor probably ca. 107 and proconsul in Asia the following year (*MRR* 1.551, 552, note 3, 553). According to Cicero he would have attained the consulship if he had not chanced upon the period of the continuous series held by Marius and the limitation they caused (*Brut.* 175: *homo per se magnus prope simili ratione summus evaserat; qui consul factus esset nisi in Marianos consulatus et in eas petitionis angustias incidisset*). Sumner interprets this passage to mean that he was a candidate for the consulship, perhaps more than once, in the period from 104 to 101, and was defeated (*Orators* 105). See Wiseman, *New Men*, 217, no. 69; and Richard J. Evans, "Missing Consuls, 104–100 B.C. A Study in Prosopography," *LCM* 10 (1985) 76–77.

8. *Q. Caecilius Metellus Macedonicus* (94) Pr. 148

In spite of the very considerable and well-recognized achievements of Metellus Macedonicus in Macedonia and Greece during and after his praetorship, and his triumph (*MRR* 1.461, 464, and 487), he was defeated for the consulships of both 145 and 144. According to the Auctor *De Viris*

---

[10]Ascon. 75C: *P. Sullam et M. Autronium significat, quorum alterum L. Cotta, alterum L. Torquatus, qui cum haec Cicero dicebat coss. erant, ambitus damnarant et in eorum locum creati sunt;* cf. Cic. *Sulla* 49–50, which, with Cic. *Fin.* 2.62, shows that Asconius is mistaken and the prosecutor was not the consul but his son; cf. also Sall. *Cat.* 18.2; Liv. *Per.* 101; and note Cic. *Sull.* 49: *ereptum repetere vos* (Cotta and Torquatus) *clamitabatis ut victi in campo in foro vinceretis.* See Marshall, *Asconius*, 261–262; *MRR* 2.157. and for another view on the elections, E. W. Gray, *Antichthon* 13 (1979) 56–67.

Illustribus (61.3), his stern and severe personality (*severitas*) repelled the voters, and still made difficult his success in finally winning election in 143.[11] He was elected censor in 131 (*MRR* 1.500).

8a. *C. Caecilius Metellus Caprarius* (84) Pr. by 117 or 116

Velleius terms Metellus Caprarius a candidate for the consulate (1.11.7; *candidatus consulatus*) at the time of the death of his father Macedonicus in 115. If Shatzman is right in dating that death early in the year, Caprarius may either have withdrawn from competing or have been defeated in the elections for 114, as he was consul in 113.[12]

9. *Q. Caecilius Metellus Numidicus* (97) Cos. 109

Plutarch (*Marius* 28.4–6), quoting as his source Rutilius Rufus, a contemporary of Marius and admittedly his enemy, records that Marius when competing in 101 for his sixth consulship, secured the defeat of a "Metellus" and the election of his rival, L. Valerius Flaccus (176) ("more a servant than a colleague"), by profuse expenditures and buying of votes.[13] As this Metellus is described as a leader whom Marius feared, to whom he had been ungrateful, and whom he was scheming with Saturninus and Glaucia to remove from Rome, the evidence points convincingly to Numidicus. The series of consulships held in succession by Marius probably removed the objection that Numidicus' first one was less than ten years before; and his censorship, if begun early in 102 (*MRR* 1.567), almost certainly ended in 101 in time for him to compete for a second consulship in 100.[14] His defeat removed a barrier to the passage of the agrarian law of Saturninus and the tumultuous activities of Saturninus and Glaucia in 100 (*MRR* 1.574, 575–576).

---

[11]Auct. *de Viris Ill.* 61.3: *Invisus plebi ob nimium severitatem et ideo post duas repulsas consul aegre factus;* Val. Max. 7.5.4: *pauci et maesti amici consulatus repulsa adflictum et rubore plenum domum reduxerant.*

[12]Other sources merely call him a *praetorius* at the time of his father's death (Cic. *Phil.* 8.14; *Fin.* 5.82; Val. Max. 7.1.1; Plin. *NH* 7.142); while Plutarch, *Fort. Rom.* 4, calls all four sons of Macedonicus consulars. See I. Shatzman, *Anc. Soc.* 5 (1974) 207.

[13]Plut., *Marius* 28.8 (Ziegler): ὡς δὲ Ῥουτίλιος ἱστορεῖ, τὰ μὲν ἄλλα φιλαλήθης ἀνὴρ καὶ χρηστός, ἰδίᾳ δὲ τῷ Μαρίῳ προσκεκρουκώς, ὥς φησι, καὶ τῆς ἕκτης ἔτυχεν ὑπατείας ἀργύριον εἰς τὰς φυλὰς καταβαλὼν πολὺ καὶ πριάμενος τὸ Μέτελλον ἐκκροῦσαι τῆς ἀρχῆς, Οὐαλλέριον δὲ Φλάκκον ὑπηρέτην μᾶλλον ἢ συνάρχοντα τῆς ὑπατείας λαβεῖν.

[14]His candidacy for a second consulship is generally accepted. See W. Schur, *Klio* 31 (1938) 313–322, esp. 313–314; Weynand, *RE* 14, Sup. 6, Col. 1399; T. F. Carney, *A Biography of Marius,* 40–41, and note 103; and Richard J. Evans, *AClass* 30 (1987) 65–68.

10. *M. Calidius* (4) Pr. 57

A candidate for the consulship of 50, M. Calidius, a leading orator in his time, was defeated by the election of L. Aemilius Paullus (61) and C. Claudius Marcellus (216). Cf. Caelius Rufus in Cic. *Fam.* 8.4.1: *M. Calidius ab repulsa postulatum.* Shackleton Bailey has shown that in Cic. *Att.* 5.19.3 and 6.8.3 Cicero refers to Calidius, not to Lucilius Hirrus, and suggests that the latter passage,[15] which is dated to October 1, 50, may refer to a second candidacy and defeat, this time for the consulship of 49 (*CLA* 3, App. II, pp. 314–315). See Marshall, *Asconius*, 128.

11. *L. Cassius Longinus* (64) Pr. 66

A candidate for the consulship of 63, Cassius is named by Asconius as one of Cicero's six competitors, and is ranked with C. Antonius (19) as a plebeian *nobilis*.[16] In the *Commentariolum Petitionis* (7), he is named with P. Sulpicius Galba (55) as an unlikely candidate. In 63 he supported Catiline, and was condemned to death on the motion of D. Iunius Silanus (163), consul designate for 62.[17] See Marshall, *Asconius*, 282, 284. On Galba, see below, No. 34.

12. *L. Cornelius Lentulus Niger* (254) Pr. by 61, Flamen Martialis

A candidate for the consulship of 58, Lentulus Niger was defeated by the election of A. Gabinius (11) and L. Calpurnius Piso (80), the candidates supported by the so-called First Triumvirate and the tribune P. Vatinius (3).[18]

13. *L. Cornelius Scipio (Asiaticus)* (337) Pr. 195

A candidate for the consulship of 191, L. Scipio competed with two patricians, P. Cornelius Scipio Nasica (350), his cousin, and Cn. Manlius Vulso (91), for the one patrician place (Liv. 35.24.4–5). P. Scipio and M'. Acilius Glabrio (35) who had both been defeated the previous year (see be-

---

[15]Cf. Cic. *Att.* 6.8.3: *Sed heus tu! Numquid moleste fers de illo qui se solet anteferre patruo sororis tuae filii? At a quibus victus!*

[16]Ascon. 82C: *duos nobiles, C. Antonium, M. Antoni oratoris filium, L. Cassium Longinum;* cf. *Comm. Pet.* 7: *Nam P. Galbam et L. Cassium, summo loco natos, quis est qui consulatum petere putet?* See Marshall, *Asconius*, 282.

[17]Cic. *Cat.* 3.9, 14, 16, 25, 4.73; Sall. *Cat.* 17.5, 44.2, 50.4.

[18]Cic. *Vat.* 12: *L. Lentulum, hunc iudicem nostrum, Flaminem Martialem, quod erat eo tempore Gabini tui competitor eiusdem Vetti indicio opprimere voluisti;* cf. Cic. *Att.* 2.24.2, and SB, *CLA* 1.398–399. See also W. C. Grummel, *CJ* 49 (1953–54) 351–355.

low, No. 14; and above, No. 1) were elected.[19] L. Scipio was elected consul the next year, for 190 (*MRR* 1.356).

14. *P. Cornelius Scipio Nasica* (350) Pr. 194

A candidate for the consulship of 192, Scipio Nasica faced intense competition from the patricians Cn. Manlius Vulso (91) and L. Quinctius Flamininus (45) for the one patrician place, as well as from four leading plebeians (Liv. 35.10.1–10). Much to Livy's surprise, since a Cornelius (Merula) also presided over the election,[20] Scipio Nasica was defeated by L. Quinctius, who was elected along with Cn. Domitius Ahenobarbus (18). He won easily the next year. See above, No. 13, on L. Scipio (377).

15. *Q. Cornificius* (7) Pr. by 66

Cornificius was one of the weaker candidates for the consulship of 63 (Cic. *Att.* 1.1.1). On him and on C. Licinius Sacerdos (154) Asconius (82C) remarks: *duos qui tantum non primi ex familiis suis magistratum adepti erant*. See SB, *CLA* 1.290; Wiseman, *New Men*, 227, no. 139; Marshall, *Asconius* 282–283.

16. *Q. Fabius Labeo* (91) Pr. 189

A candidate for the consulship of 184, Labeo was one of the three competing patricians in Livy's account (39.32.6–13) whom he describes as *veteres candidatos*, and who were all defeated by P. Claudius Pulcher (305). See above, on L. Aemilius Paullus (114), No. 4. There is no mention of the date of his previous candidacy, but it must have been later than 188. He was elected to the consulship of 183 (*MRR* 1.378).

17. *D. Iunius Silanus* (163) Pr. by 67

Cicero mentions Silanus as a rival of a certain Thermus for the consulship of 64 (*Att.* 1.1.2). Thermus was very probably the C. Marcius Figulus (65) who was elected, along with L. Iulius Caesar (145), to the consulship of that

---

[19]Note Liv. 35.24.5: *P. Scipioni, ut dilatum viro tali non negatum honorem appareret, consulatus datus est.* See Briscoe, *Comm.* 2, p. 180; MRR 1.352.

[20]Liv. 35.10.1–10, esp. 9: *his obtinuit ut praeferretur* (L. Quinctius) *candidato quem Africanus frater ducebat, quem Cornelia gens Cornelio consule comitia habente.* See Briscoe, *Comm.* 2, pp. 158–159.

year, a Q. Minucius Thermus adopted by a Marcius Figulus.[21] It is not known whether Silanus continued his candidacy or withdrew. He was elected to the consulship of 62
(*MRR* 2.172–173).

18. *C. Laelius* (2) Pr. 196

Laelius was a candidate in the hotly contested election for
the consulships of 192 (Liv. 35.30.5–10; see above, No. 1, on
M'. Acilius Glabrio [35]). He was defeated,[22] in spite of direct
support from Scipio Africanus, by Cn. Domitius Ahenobarbus (18), but was elected two years later to the consulship of
190, with L. Scipio, brother of Africanus, as his colleague
(*MRR* 1.356).

19. *C. Laelius Sapiens* (3) Pr. 145

The younger Laelius was a candidate for the consulship of
141, but was defeated by Q. Pompeius (2), the first Pompeius to attain the office. The close friend and supporter of
Laelius, Scipio Aemilianus, thereupon renounced his friend-
ship for Pompeius because he was soliciting support for
himself while Scipio, his patron, and Laelius were expecting
support from him.[23] Laelius won election to the consulship
of 140, the next year (*MRR* 1.479).

20. *C. Licinius Sacerdos* (154) Pr. 75

An unsuccessful candidate for the consulship of 63, undistinguished but not *novus* (Asconius 82C). See above, No.
15, on Q. Cornificius (7). See Wiseman, *New Men*, 237, No.
225; cf. *MRR* 3.124. There is no record of a candidacy between his praetorship in 75 and the elections for 63. See
Marshall, *Asconius*, 283.

---

[21]This conjecture is based on the preservation of the names *Caesare et Turmo* by the
Chronographer of 354 as consuls of 64. It was favored by Drumann-Groebe (*RG*² 5,431)
but doubted by Münzer (*RE* s.v. Minucius, No. 60). It is accepted by SB, *CLA* 1.292, and
Two Studies, 121–122. E. W. Gray offers the explanation that a Minucius Thermus was
elected but condemned, and a Marcius Figulus was elected to his place in a second
election (*Antichthon* 13 [1979] 56–65). But there is no other evidence that there was a
second election.

[22]Liv. 35.10.10: *adeo ne in plebeio quidem consule, cum pro C. Laelio niteretur, Africanus
valuit.* On the patrician whom Africanus also supported, see above, No. 14, on Scipio
Nasica (350), and note 20.

[23]Cic. *Lael.* 77; Plut. *Apophth. Scip. Min.* 8 (Mor. 172A). See *MRR* 1.477. On the quarrel
with Pompeius, see A. E. Astin, *Scipio Aemilianus,* 122–123, and 311–312.

21. *C. Livius Salinator* (29) Pr. 202

An unsuccessful candidate in the hotly contested election for the consulship of 192 (Liv. 35.10.3; see above, No. 1, on M'. Acilius Glabrio). He may be the C. Livius Salinator who held a second praetorship in 191 (Liv. 35.24.6; *MRR* 1.353), won a victory over the fleet of Antiochus the Great, and was elected to the consulship of 188 (Liv. 38.35.1; *MRR* 1.365).[24]

22. *L. Lucceius Q. f.* (6) Pr. 67

A candidate for the consulship of 59 (Cic. *Att.* 1.14.7, 17.11; cf. Asconius 91C). He allied himself with his fellow candidate, C. Iulius Caesar, but was defeated by Caesar's rival and enemy, M. Calpurnius Bibulus (Suet. *Caes.* 19; see *MRR* 2.187).[25] No other candidacy of his is recorded.

23. *Q. Lutatius Catulus* (7) Pr. by 109

As a candidate for the consulship, Catulus, a member of a plebeian family prominent since the First Punic War, was defeated three times. Cicero mentions all three in the *Pro Plancio* in a series of examples ostensibly intended to show Iuventius Laterensis, the prosecutor of Plancius, and himself the defeated candidate for the curule aedileship (see below, Aediles, No. 5), how unstable and unpredictable the popular elections really were. Catulus was defeated first for the consulship of 106 by C. Atilius Serranus (64), "a *nobilis*, but utterly stupid" (Cic. *Planc.* 12; *MRR* 1.553), second, for the consulship of 105 by C. Mallius Maximus (13), "not merely ignoble, but mean and contemptible" (*Planc.* 12; cf. *Mur.* 56; *MRR* 1.555), and third, for the consulship of 104 by C. Flavius Fimbria (87), "a *novus homo*, and a man of spirit and sense."[26] Catulus was at last elected for the consulship

---

[24]Weissenborn has drawn attention to the bit of uncertainty aroused because Livy in 35.24.6 does not note that his praetorship in 191 was a second one. See Briscoe, *Comm.* 1, pp. 180–181.

[25]On the dispute whether the L. Lucceius who was a candidate for the consulship of 59 was the L. Lucceius Q. f. named above or L. Lucceius M. f. (5), a Roman business man, active in Italy and the East, and known to Cicero, see SB, *CLF* 1.318–319; and *MRR* 3.127–128; and, in favor of M. f., W. C. McDermott, *Hermes* 97 (1969) 233–246. A passage in Asconius (91C)—*L. Lucceius, paratus eruditusque, qui postea consulatum quoque petiit*—is strongly in favor of Q. f., the historian. See also Marshall, *Asconius*, 284–285 (on the *coitio*), 288, 309; and G. R. Stanton and B. A. Marshall, *Historia* 24 (1975) 215–218.

[26]Cic. *Planc.* 12: *Praeposuisse se Q. Catulo. summa in familia nato, sapientissimo et sanctissimo viro, non dico C. Serranum, stultissimum hominem—fuit enim tamen nobilis—, non C. Fimbriam, novum hominem—fuit enim animi satis magni et consili—, sed Cn. Mallium. non*

of 102 with Marius as his colleague at a time when the final struggle with the Cimbri and the Teutones was imminent (*MRR* 1.567).

24. *L. Manlius Torquatus* (79) Pr. by 68

When a candidate for the consulship of 65, Torquatus was defeated in the regular election by the patrician, P. Cornelius Sulla (386), but after the conviction of the two victors, Sulla and Autronius Paetus (see above, No. 6, on L. Aurelius Cotta [102]) for *ambitus,* he and his colleague Cotta were successful in the ensuing second election.

25. *Cn. Manlius Vulso* (91) Pr. 195

A candidate for the consulship of 192 (Liv. 35.10.2), Manlius was defeated by the election of L. Quinctius Flamininus (43) and Cn. Domitius Ahenobarbus (18). He was again a candidate the next year for the consulship of 191, with L. Cornelius Scipio (337) and P. Cornelius Scipio Nasica (350) as competitors for the one patrician place, which Nasica won (Liv. 35.24.4–5; see above, No. 13, on L. Cornelius Scipio [377]). Manlius was finally elected to the consulship of 189 (*MRR* 1.360). See also Briscoe, *Comm.* 2, 180.

26. *C. Marcius Figulus* (62)

A prominent jurisconsult, Marcius Figulus, was a defeated candidate for the consulship in an unknown year. Valerius Maximus records that, stung by his defeat, he dismissed with a rebuke the crowd that came to consult him the next day.[27] As he was a son of the consul of the same name who held office in 162 and 156 (*MRR* 1.441, 447), his candidacy and the incident may be dated about 130 B.C. See W. Kunkel, *Herkunft und Sociale Stellung der römischen Juristen*, p. 14, no. 22.

---

solum ignobilem virum sine virtute, sine ingenio, vita etiam contempta et sordida. On Mallius, cf. also Cic. *Mur.* 36: *Quis Q. Catulum humanitate, sapientia, integritate antecellentem a Cn. Mallio (superari posse arbitratus est)?*

[27]Val. Max. 9.3.2: *Caium autem Figulum mansuetissimum. pacato iuris civilis iudicio celeberrimum, prudentiae moderationisque immemorem (iracundiae stimuli) reddiderunt. Consulatus enim repulsa dolore accensus, eo quidem magis quod illum bis patri suo datum meminerat, cum ad eum postero comitiorum die multi consulendi causa venissent, omnes dimisit, praefatus "An vos consulere scitis, consulem facere nescitis?"*

27. *L. Marcius Philippus* (75) Pr. by 96

A candidate for the consulship of 93, he was defeated by C. Valerius Flaccus (168), and, most surprisingly, by M. Herennius (10).[28] He was elected consul for 91, and to the censorship in 86 (*MRR* 2.20, and 54).

28. *L. Opimius* (4) Pr. 125

A candidate for the consulship of 122, Opimius was defeated when Gaius Gracchus, then tribune of the plebs (*MRR* 1.513, 517), gave his support to C. Fannius M. f. (7) (Plut. *CG* 8.2; 11.2–3). As the influence of Gracchus declined during the following year, Opimius won election to the consulship of 121 (*MRR* 1.520).

29. *M. Porcius Cato* (16) Pr. 54

A candidate for the consulship of 51, Cato damaged his own chances by persuading the Senate to decree the restriction of canvassing to personal meetings, and by refusing to engage in the usual greetings that might win good will and votes (what in the *Commentariolum petitionis* [11] is called *diligentia petendi*), and so was defeated (Plut. *Cato Min.* 49–50; Dio 40.58).[29] Ser. Sulpicius Rufus (95) and M. Claudius Marcellus (229) were elected (*MRR* 2.240–241).

30. *L. Porcius Licinus* (23) Pr. 193

The successful one of the three plebeian candidates for the consulship of 184 (*MRR* 1.374; see above, No. 4, on L. Aemilius Paullus), Porcius Licinus is shown by Livy's description of them (39.32.8: *et hi repulsis in spem impetrandi tandem aliquando honoris dilati*) to have been defeated in a previous election. It must have been between 191 and 185, but there is no record of the year.

---

[28]Cic. *Mur.* 36: *Quis L. Philippum, summo ingenio, opere, gratia, nobilitate, a M. Herenni superari posse arbitratus est? Brut.* 166: *M. Herennius in mediocribus oratoribus Latine et diligenter loquentibus numeratus est, qui tamen summa nobilitate hominem, cognatione, sodalitate, collegio, summa etiam eloquentia L. Philippum in consulatus petitione superavit.* Note in *Mur.* 36, Cicero's comment on popular elections: *nihil est incertius vulgo, nihil obscurius voluntate hominum, nihil fallacius ratione toto comitiorum.*

[29]On Cato's reception of his defeat, see Seneca, *Epp. Mor.* 104.35: *Eodem quo repulsus est die in comitio pila lusit;* cf. Plut. *Cat. Min,* 50.1; cf. R. Fehrle, *Cato Uticensis,* 214–218.

31. *L. Rupilius* (14) Pr. by 133

A candidate for the consulship in some year between 132, when his brother, P. Rupilius (5), was consul, and the death of Scipio Aemilianus in 129, L. Rupilius was defeated in spite of the patronage of Scipio, who had secured the success of his brother (Cic. *Lael*, 73). Cicero and Pliny report that his brother died, overwhelmed with grief at his defeat.[30]

32. *P. Rutilius Rufus* (34) Pr. by 118

A candidate for the consulship of 115, Rutilius Rufus was defeated by M. Aemilius Scaurus (140) and M. Cacecilius Metellus (77). Rutilius then prosecuted Scaurus for *ambitus*, and Scaurus, when acquitted, in turn prosecuted him.[31] There is no record that Rutilius was again a candidate in the long interval between 115 and his election to the consulship of 105 (*MMR* 1.555).

33. *L. Sergius Catilina* (23) Pr. 68

Catiline's intention to compete for a consulship was evident from the time of his governorship of Africa in 67, but rejection of his *professio* in 66 prevented his candidacy for 65, and his trial for extortion in 65 prevented it also for 64. See below, Part 2, No. 24. According to Asconius (82C), when he was at last free in 64 to compete for 63, there were seven candidates, two patricians, Catiline himself and P. Sulpicius Galba (55; see below, No. 34), and four plebeians, two of whom, C. Antonius (19) and L. Cassius Longinus (64; see above, No. 11), were *nobiles*, and two, Q. Cornificius (7; see above, No. 15) and C. Licinius Sacerdos (154; see above, No. 20) were worthy but undistinguished. And there was M. Tullius Cicero (29), a *novus homo*. Catiline arranged a combination (*coitio*) with Antonius, and with support from Crassus and Caesar became Cicero's chief rival (Ascon. 82–83C).

---

[30]Cic. *Tusc.* 4.40: *Aegre tulisse P. Rupilius fratris repulsam consulatus scriptum apud Fannium est. quippe qui ob eam causam e vita recesserit, moderatius igitur ferre debuit; Lael.* 73: *non enim neque tu possis, quamvis excellas, omnes tuos ad honores amplissimos perducere, ut Scipio P. Rupilium potuit consulem efficere, fratrem eius Lucium non potuit;* cf. Plin. *NH* 7.122: *P. Rupilius morbo levi impeditus nuntiata fratris repulsa in consulatus petitione ilico expiravit;* cf. Peter, *HRR* 1, p. 139.

[31]Cic. *Brut.* 113: *Erat uterque* (Rutilius and Scaurus) *natura vehemens et acer: itaque cum una consulatum petivissent, non ille solum, qui repulsam tulerat, accusavit ambitus designatum competitorem, sed Scaurus etiam absolutus Rutilium in iudicium vocavit;* cf. *De Or.* 2.280; cf. Tac. *Ann.* 3.66. See Marshall, *Asconius*, 124–125.

His radical program, and the weakness of the other candidates, brought strong conservative support to Cicero (Ascon. 94C: *consul omnium consensu factus est*), while C. Antonius, probably aided by the memory of his father, the distinguished orator, M. Antonius (28), received the votes of a few more centuries than Catiline and was elected (Ascon.: *pauculis centuriis Catilinam superavit;* cf. Sall. *Cat.* 21.1–24.1).

Defeated for 63, Catiline was again a candidate the next year, for 62, and competed with at least three others: Servius Sulpicius Rufus (95), the famous jurist (below, No. 37), who was defeated, and the two who were successful, D. Iunius Silanus (163) and L. Licinius Murena (123) (*MRR* 2.172). While competing, Catiline was at the same time arming forces, and plotting attacks on the consul Cicero (Sall. *Cat.* 26.1: *omnibus modis insidias parabat Ciceroni*), while the latter aroused feeling against him by wearing a breastplate and having the protection of an armed guard of friends during the election (Sall. *Cat.* 26.4; *Mur.* 52; Dio 37.29). It was after this defeat that Catiline turned fully to armed rebellion. See E. G. Hardy, *JRS* 7 (1917) 153–228, esp. 157–162, 166–172, 178–185; M. Gelzer, *RE* II A, 1697–1704; Marshall, *Asconius*, 281–283, 317–318; A. Kaplan, *Catiline; The Man and his Role in the Roman Revolution*, 51–61.

33a. *? P. Servilius Vatia (Isauricus)* (93)

Servilius Vatia held a praetorship, probably in 90 B.C., and his triumph *pro praetore* in 88 from an unknown province, perhaps Spain or Sardinia, was recorded in the *Acta Triumphalia* (A. Degrassi, *Inscr. Ital.* 13.1.84 f., 563; see *MRR* 2.25, 30, note 4, 35, 43). Plutarch (*Sulla* 10.2–4) mentions that in 88 two candidates for offices (*archai*) whom Sulla preferred, one named Servaeus and the other named Nonius, a nephew of Sulla, were rejected by the people because of Sulla's unpopularity. Mommsen's emendation of Servaeus to Servilius was accepted by Drumann-Groebe (*RG*² II, 559) amd Münzer (*RE* IIA, 1812, and *APF* 303). If it is correct, the future Isauricus, the most probable identification, was a defeated candidate for the consulship of 87, when another patrician, L. Cornelius Cinna, was elected (*MRR* 2.45). In 80, after Sulla's victory, Servilius was elected for 79 (*MRR* 2.82). On Nonius, see below, Tribunes of the Plebs, No. 6.

34. *P. Sulpicius Galba* (55) Pr. by 66

A patrician candidate for the consulship of 63, Galba is described by Asconius (82C) as *sobrius et sanctus*, while Cicero (*Att.* 1.1.1, dated to July of 65) was sure he would compete but noted that his canvassing was meeting with flat refusals. Galba was one of the four, Galba, Cassius, Cornificius, and Licinius Sacerdos, *qui prope iacebant.*[32] See above, No. 33, on L. Sergius Catilina.

35. Ser. Sulpicius Galba (57) Pr. 187

A candidate for the consulship of 184, Galba had also been one for a previous year as he was one of the three patricians whom Livy calls *veteres candidatos* (39.32.6). As he had held a praetorship in 187, he must have been a candidate in 186 for the consulship of 185. See above, No. 4, on L. Aemilius Paullus (114).

36. Ser. Sulpicius Galba (61) Pr. 54

This Galba, a former legatus of Caesar in Gaul (*MRR* 2.199, 205, 212), was a candidate, apparently with Caesar's support, for the consulship of 49, but was defeated by the election of two of Caesar's opponents, C. Claudius Marcellus (217) and L. Cornelius Lentulus Crus (218).[33] He had been elected an augur before 49 (Cic. *Att.* 9.9.3). He was one of the conspirators against Caesar (cf. Cic. *Phil.* 13.33), and in 43 served as a legate under Hirtius and as an envoy for Decimus Brutus (*MRR* 2.351, 355).

37. Ser. Sulpicius Rufus (95) Pr. 65

Prominent as a jurisconsult, Ser. Sulpicius Rufus competed for the consulship of 62, but was defeated by the election of D. Iunius Silanus (163) and L. Licinius Murena (125). See *MRR* 2.172. With support from Cato the Younger, Sul-

---

[32]Cic. *Att.* 1.1.1: *prensat unus P. Galba; sine fuco et fallaciis more maiorum negatur;* cf. *Comm. Pet.* 7. See SB, *CLA* 1.289. He had been coopted as a pontifex by 69 (L. R. Taylor, *AJPh* 63 [1942] 385–412), and is named as one in 57 (Cic. *Har. Resp.* 12). He may possibly be the *praetorius* who was killed by mutinous soldiers of Caesar in 47 (Plut. *Caes.* 5.1; cf. SB, *CLA* 1.289). See also Marshall, *Asconius,* 281; W. C. Grummel, *CJ* 49 (1953–54) 351–354.

[33]Hirtius in Caes. *BG* 8.50.3: *propterea quod insolenter adversarii sui gloriarentur L. Lentulum et C. Marcellum consules creatos qui omnem honorem et dignitatem Caesaris spoliarent, ereptum Ser. Galbae consulatum, cum is multo plus gratia suffragii valuisset, quod sibi coniunctus ex familiaritate et necessitudine legationis esset.* References to his relations with Caesar in 49 (Cic. *Att.* 9.9.3), and again in 47 (*Fam.* 6.18.3; Val. Max. 6.2.11), indicate that Suetonius is mistaken in making this defeat the reason why he turned against Caesar and joined the conspirators (*Galba* 3.2: *ob repulsam consulatus infensus Iulio Caesari cuius legatus in Gallis fuerat, conspiravit cum Cassio et Bruto, propter quod Pedia lege damnatus est.*) See Münzer, *RE* s.v. Sulpicius No. 61; SB, *CLA* 4.375. and *CLF* 2.385.

picius prosecuted Murena for *ambitus*, but Cicero defended him and won his acquittal (Cic. *Mur. passim*). Cicero mentions Sulpicius in a letter to Atticus late in April, 59, as a possible candidate for the consulship of 58 (*Att.* 2.5.2; SB, *CLA* 1.361), but there is no evidence that he became a candidate either then or before he stood for the consulship of 51 (*MRR* 2.240–241).[34] See Marshall, *Asconius*, 139, 176–177.

38. *Q. Terentius Culleo* (53) Pr. 187

A candidate for the consulship of 184, with four patricians and two other plebeians as rivals, Terentius was defeated by the election of P. Claudius Pulcher (305) and L. Porcius Licinus (23) (Liv. 39.32.8). See above, No. 4, on L. Aemilius Paullus (114). Livy indicates that all the plebeian candidates had stood before. Terentius, a praetor in 187, must previously have tried and been defeated for the consulship of 185 when Ap. Claudius Pulcher (294) and M. Sempronius (85) were elected (Liv. 39.23.2). See above, No. 7. on Cn. Baebius Tamphilus (141).

39. *L. Turius* (2) Pr. 75

A candidate for the consulship of 64, Turius, though a *novus homo* or of a recently senatorial family, fell short of election by only a few centuries (Cic. *Brut.* 237: *paucae centuriae ad consulatum defuerunt;* cf. *Att.* 1.1.2).[35] L. Iulius Caesar (145) and C. Marcius Figulus (65) were elected consuls for 64 (*MRR* 2.161).

40. *? C. Valerius Flaccus* (168) Pr. by 96

Observing that nobles who had been defeated candidates in one election year had often been successful the following year, E. Badian suggested that, of the two distinguished nobles who were candidates for the consulship of 94, the one who was defeated by the *novus homo*, C. Coelius Caldus (12),

---

[34]Plutarch (*Cat. Min.* 49.2) remarks that Sulpicius was criticized when he was a candidate for the consulship in 52 for not withdrawing in favor of his competitor Cato in gratitude for the aid he had received from Cato in the past. See above, No. 29, on M. Porcius Cato (16).

[35]On the name and the identity of the praetor of 75 who is thought to be Turius, the later candidate for the consulship, perhaps of 64, see SB, *CLA* 1.292–293; Wiseman, *New Men*, 267, no. 448; Sumner, *Orators*, 127, Marshall, *Asconius*, 316–317; *MRR* 3.209–210.

was C. Valerius Flaccus (168), who was elected the next year as consul for 93 (*Studies*, 94–95, 103–104, note 159).[36]

41. *M. Valerius Messalla* (252) Pr. 193

A candidate for the consulship of 189, Valerius Messalla had as competitors the plebeian M. Fulvius Nobilior (91) and two patricians, Cn. Manlius Vulso (91) and M. Aemilius Lepidus (68). He was badly defeated (*Nam Messalla iacuit*), while Fulvius and finally Manlius were elected (Liv. 37.47.6–8; *MRR* 1.360). He won the consulship the following year for 188 (Liv. 38.35.1; *MRR* 1.365). On these elections, see above, No. 2. on M. Aemilius Lepidus (68).

2. Candidates Who Withdrew or Were Prevented from Competing

1. *Q. Aelius Paetus* (103) Pontifex

Paetus was a candidate for the consulship of 216, in the *interregnum* at the beginning of that consular year, in competition with three patricians, P. Cornelius Merenda (266; see below, No. 11), L. Manlius Vulso (92; see below, No. 18), and M. Aemilius Lepidus (67; see below, No. 2), and two other plebeians, C. Atilius Serranus (62; see below, No. 7), and C. Terentius Varro (83). At first, although all competed, only Varro secured election as none of the others received a majority of the centuries, and so took office at once and became responsible for the election of a colleague. According to Livy (22.34–35), the *nobilitas*, believing that none of the others was strong enough for so critical a time in the war with Hannibal, pressed L. Aemilius Paullus (118; Cos. 219), though unwilling, to become a candidate on the next comitial day. All who had competed with Varro withdrew, and Paullus was elected.[37] Paetus died in the battle of Cannae (Liv. 23.21.7).

---

[36]*Comm. Pet.* 11: *Ille* (C. Coelius) *cum duobus hominibus ita nobilissimis petebat ut tamen in iis omnia pluris esset quam ipsa nobilitas, summa ingenia, summus pudor, plurima beneficia, summa ratio ac diligentia petendi; ac tamen eorum alterum Coelius, cum multo inferior erat genere, superior nulla re paene, superavit.*

[37]There has been much discussion of Livy's account of the consular elections for 216, some expressing doubt of its reliability as a whole or in regard to various details, and some rallying to its defense. See the titles listed by G. V. Sumner, "Elections at Rome in 217 B.C.," *Phoenix* 29 (1975) 250, note 1. There is no mention of the *interregnum* in the *Fasti Capitolini*. The series of events is extremely complicated, consuls who both feel unable, even at the Senate's request, to come to Rome to hold the elections without endangering public safety, the dictator named by a consul is found to be *vitio creatus*, and

2. *M. Aemilius Lepidus* (67) Pr. 218

Lepidus was a candidate for the consulship of 216, who failed of election with C. Terentius Varro (83), and withdrew when L. Aemilius Paullus (119) became a candidate (Liv. 22.34–35). See above, No. 1, on Q. Aelius Paetus (103). Lepidus may have been elected a praetor suffectus in 216, and was a praetor again in 213 (*MRR* 1.249 and 253, note 2; 263 and 266, notes 1 and 2).

3. *M. Aemilius Regillus* (128) Flamen Martialis

Aemilius Regillus was a candidate for the consulship of 214, along with T. Otacilius Crassus (12; see below, No. 21), but when these two received the vote of the *centuria praerogativa*, Aniensis iuniorum, Fabius Maximus the Cunctator, the presiding consul, stopped proceedings, and urged them to vote for commanders who would be a better match for Hannibal, this without regard for the furious objections of Otacilius, who was his son-in-law. In a second vote the *centuria* named Fabius himself and M. Claudius Marcellus (220). They were elected, Fabius to his fourth consulship and Marcellus to his third (Liv. 24.7.10–9.6; *MRR* 1.258–259). Livy mentions no other candidates.

4. *M. Aemilius Scaurus* (141) Pr. 56

Scaurus, son of the famous consul of 115 and princeps senatus, was a candidate for the consulship of 53, with C. Memmius (8; see below, No. 20), Cn. Domitius Calvinus (43; Supb. 3, col. 594), and another patrician, M. Valerius Messalla (Rufus) (268). as competitors. He was prosecuted in 54 for extortion in his province, Sardinia, and upon acquittal on September 2 (see Asconius 18–20C), he engaged, like his rivals, in massive bribery, and, like them, was pros-

---

finally an *interregnum* in which only one consul secures election, and the apparent weakness of the other candidates leads to the "drafting" of a stronger and more experienced commander in Aemilius Paullus while the others withdraw. The use of conflicts between patricians and plebeians to explain changes and delays seems anachronistic. De Sanctis found much of the detail unreliable but accepted the *interregnum* and saw in the outcome a decision in favor of immediate aggressive action against Hannibal (*Storia dei Romani* 3.2.55–56, notes 88 and 89). Sumner (see above) rejects the *interregnum*, and with it the order of the elections, but E. S. Gruen (*CSCA* 11 [1978] 61–74) and B. L. Twyman (*CPh* 79 [1984] 285–294), while admitting the anachronisms, hold that the basic facts are reliable, and see a sufficient explanation for the series of changes and delays in the conflict between those who favored prompt and aggressive action against Hannibal and those who favored a continuance of a Fabian strategy. The result of the election was a victory for the former.

ecuted for *ambitus,* while his candidacy failed.[38] Cicero again came to his defense (Quint. *Inst. Or.* 4.1.68), but he was convicted in 52 under a law that Pompey had carried as sole consul (App. *BC* 2.24), and had no further career. Domitius Calvinus and Valerius Messalla were finally elected in July of 53 (*MRR* 2.227–228; 3.214) after an excessively long *interregnum.*

5. *T. Annius Milo (Papianus)* (67) Pr. 55

A candidate for the consulate of 52, Milo competed with P. Plautius Hypsaeus (23; see below, No. 22) and Q. Caecilius Metellus Scipio (99). P. Clodius Pulcher (48), his enemy, competing for a praetorship in 52, and a supporter of Hypsaeus and Scipio, opposed Milo bitterly in the belief that as consul he would curb and weaken his praetorship. Both engaged in profuse expenditure and were attended by armed bands. Their strife prevented the holding of elections for 52 in 53, and the creation of interreges early in 52, and reached its climax when Clodius was murdered by Milo's guards on January 18 in a clash at Bovillae. Disorders, which included the burning of the Curia, led to the election of Pompey as sole consul. Under Pompey's new legislation Milo was tried and convicted *de vi,* though Cicero spoke in his defense. He went into exile at Massilia, convicted in absence also *de ambitu* and *de sodaliciis.* See Asconius 30–56C, Cicero, *Pro*

---

[38]Scaurus and Memmius appear to have had at first some support from the "Triumvirate," Scaurus from Pompey and Memmius from Caesar, but it failed in the profuse bribery and the extraordinary election scandals, including a scandalous bargain between the consuls in office and two of the candidates, Memmius and Domitius. See *Att.* 4.16.6 (ca. July 1): *Memmius Censaris commendetur militibus, Pompei gratia nitatur; Att.* 4.15.7 (July 27): *Memmium Caesaris omnes opes confirmant. Cum eo Domitium consules iunxerunt, qua pactione epistulae committere iam non audeo. Pompeius fremit, queritur, Scauro studet, sed utrum fronte an mente dubitatur;* and on the situation after Memmius, at Pompey's advice revealed the *pactio* (*Att.* 4.17.2 October 1) and made it void. See Cic. *QF* 3.6.3: *Ego Messallam Caesari praestabo, . . . Memmius in adventu Caesaris* [i.e., to Cisalpine Gaul] *habet spem, in quo illum puto errare; hic quidem friget. Scaurum autem iam pridem Pompeius abiecit.* On bribery by Scaurus, see Cic. *Att.* 4.17.4 (dated Oct. 1): *Singulis diebus usque ad pr. Kal. Oct. quo ego haec die scripsi, sublatis, populo tributim domi suae satisfecerat, sed tamen, etsi uberior liberalitas huius gratior esse videbatur eorum qui occuparant.* On the new round of prosecutions for *ambitus* in the autumn of 54, see Cic. *QF* 3.2.3, dated October 10: *De ambitu postulati sunt omnes qui consulatum petunt: a Memmio Domitius, a Q. Acutio, bono et erudito adulescente, Memmius, a Q. Pompeio Messalla, a Triario Scaurus:* and on the candidates: *consules comitia habere cupiunt; rei nolunt, et maxime Memmius, quod Caesaris adventu se sperat futurum consulem, sed mirum in modum iacet. Domitius cum Messalla certus esse videbatur. Scaurus refrixerat.* On the elections for the consulship of 53, see E. S. Gruen, "The Consular Elections for 53 B.C.," *Hommages à Marcel Renard,* Vol. II, 311–321; G. V. Sumner, "The Coitio of 54 B.C. or Waiting for Caesar," *HSPh* 86 (1983) 133–139; Marshall, *Asconius,* 121–122, 212–213; C. Henderson, Jr., "The Career of the Younger M. Aemilius Scaurus," *CJ* 53 (1957–1958) 194–206, esp. 199–200.

Milone, passim; and, on Clodius, below, Praetors, Part 2, No. 1. Note also Lintott, "Cicero and Milo," *JRS* 65 (1974) 62–78; Marshall, *Asconius,* 159–213.

5a. *? C. Aquillius Gallus* (23) Pr. 66

An eminent jurist whom Cicero mentions as a possible candidate for the consulship of 63, but one not likely to compete (*Att.* 1.1.1). See SB, *CLA* 1.290; Marshall, *Asconius,* 281; *MRR* 2.152. He is not named on Asconius' list (82C).

6. *Q. Arrius* (8, cf. 7) Pr. 73

Q. Arrius, probably the praetor of 73 (*MRR* 2.109, 117; 3.25), was a close associate of Crassus, and the man through whom L. Lucceius in 60 expected to arrange a *coitio* with Caesar in the contest for the consulship of 59 (Cic. *Att.* 1.17.11; cf. *Brut.* 242–243; SB, *CLA* 1.328–329; and above, Part 1, No. 22, on L. Lucceius). It is clear that Arrius hoped to compete for the consulship of 58, but he may never have become a candidate, since both he and Cicero were aware by April of 59 that he no longer had support from the Triumvirs.[39]

7. *C. Atilius Serranus* (62) Pr. 218

Atilius was a candidate for the consulship of 216, but withdrew after the election of Terentius Varro (83) when L. Aemilius Paullus became a candidate (Liv. 22.34–35). See above, No. 1, on Q. Aelius Paetus (103).

7a. *? T. Aufidius* (12)

Praetor in 67 or 66, and after it a successful governor of Asia (Val. Max. 6.9.7; *MRR* 2.143, 154; *AJPh* 111 [1990] 73–74), Cicero names him as an unlikely candidate for the consulship of 63 (*Att.* 1.1.1: *De Aufidio et de Palicano non puto te exspectare dum scribam*). See SB, *CLA* 1.291; Marshall, *Asconius,* 281. He is not named in Asconius' list of candidates for 63 (82C).

---

[39]See Cic. *Att.* 2.5.2: *quid Arrius narret, quo animo se destitutum ferat; Att.* 2.7.3: *iam vero Arrius consulatum sibi ereptum fremit.* On the identity of Q. Arrius, praetor in 73, with the Arrius named above, see R. J. Baker and B. A. Marshall, *Historia* 24 (1973) 220–231. See also SB, *CLA* 1, p. 328; A. M. Ward, *Marcus Crassus and the Late Roman Republic,* 85, note 43; 215, note 62; B. A. Marshall, *Crassus: A Political Biography,* 101, 105; *MRR* 3.25; W. C. Grummel, *CJ* 49 (1953–54) 351–355, esp. 352.

8. *? M. Caesonius* (3) Pr. by 66

In a letter to Atticus in July, 65, Cicero mentions Caesonius as a possible but improbable candidate for the consulship of 63.[40] Asconius makes no mention of him in his list of
the seven who competed (82C).

9. *C. Claudius Pulcher* (303) Pr. 56

Cicero in his speech *Pro Scauro* suggests that the attacks of
Ap. Claudius Pulcher (297), consul in 54, on the candidacy
of his client, M. Aemilius Scaurus (141), for the consulship
of 53 are due to the possibility that he would be a rival of C.
Claudius Pulcher, his brother, then governor of the province
of Asia, who might return to compete for 53, which would
in fact be *suus annus.*[41] But his command was extended for
another year.

10. *P. Cornelius Dolabella* (141) Tr. pl. 47

According to Cicero,[42] Caesar had promised and confirmed for Dolabella the regular consulate for 44, thus in-
ducing him to become a candidate with M. Antonius as his
colleague, and then had disappointed him by taking the
consulship himself. After Caesar's assassination Dolabella,
apparently without opposition from Antonius or the Libera-
tors, proceeded to assume the consular insignia and
authority.[43]

11. *P. Cornelius Merenda* (266)

Cornelius Merenda, a candidate for the consulship of 216,
withdrew along with the others after the election of C. Ter-

---

[40]Cic. *Att.* 1.1.1: *Ut frontem ferias, sunt qui etiam Caesonium putent.*

[41]Cic. *Scaur.* 31–36, esp. 33: *Neque vero tam haec ipsa cotidiana res Appium Claudiam illa humanitate et sapientia praeditum per se ipsa movisset nisi hunc C. Claudi, fratris sui, competi-torem putasset;* cf. Ascon. 25C. See Marshall, *Asconius,* 124, 146–147. E. Courtney points out that by the time of the trial of Scaurus (summer, 54), C. Claudius Pulcher was al-ready committed to another year as governor of Asia, and Cicero was simply seizing a pretext (*Philologus* 105 [1961] 151–156).

[42]Cic. *Phil.* 2.79: *nihil queror de Dolabella qui tum est impulsus, inductus, elusus. Qua in re quanta fuit uterque vestrum perfidia in Dolabellam quis ignorat? Ille induxit ut peteret, promis-sum et receptum intervertit, ad seque transtulit.* Caesar's action may have been due to the violent objections of Marcus Antonius. He must have intended in any case that Dola-bella should succeed him as consul upon his departure for the Parthian war. On this passage, see J. D. Denniston's *Commentary,* 144; and on the actions of Antonius as augur, J. Linderski, "The Augural Law," *ANRW* II, 16, 2198–2199.

[43]See *MRR* 2.317.

entius Varro (83) when L. Aemilius Paullus (118) became a
candidate (Liv. 22.34–35). See above, No. 1, on Q. Aelius
Paetus (103).

12. *L. Domitius Ahenobarbus* (27) Pr. 58

Domitius, as a candidate for the consulship of 55, a year
which he had good reason to consider as *suus annus*, faced
the opposition of Pompey and Crassus, who were planning
to become consuls that year themselves. Elections were delayed by trickery and violence, so that they might postpone
the announcement of their candidacies, and the elections,
and thus force an *interregnum*. As their intentions became
known, the other candidates, not named in our sources,
withdrew, but Domitius, with the support of Cato, persisted
until a slave was killed and Cato was wounded.[44] Pompey
and Crassus were elected as planned. Domitius was elected,
apparently without difficulty, to the consulship of 54 (*MRR*
2.221).

13. *Q. Fabius Maximus Rullianus* (114) Cos. 322, 310, 305, 297, 295

Fabius Rullianus, in his fourth consulship, was holding
the elections for the consulship of 296. As Livy describes it
(10.15.7–12, probably from unreliable sources), the centuries
were unanimously voting to name Rullianus consul, and his
competitor for the patrician place, the ambitious candidate,
Ap. Claudius Caecus (91), with the support of all the nobil-
ity, pressed for the restoration of both consulships to the patricians. Fabius refused and withdrew, saying that he would
have accepted the names of two patricians if he could see
another than himself made consul, but would not commit
the extremely bad precedent of illegally accepting his own
candidacy. The plebeian, L. Volumnius Flamma Violens (13),
and Appius Claudius Caecus (91) were elected consuls for
296 (*MRR* 1.176), and Fabius consul again for 295 (*MRR*
1.177).

14. *C. Iulius Caesar Strabo (Vopiscus)* (135)

C. Caesar, a brother of the consul of 90, and an orator
noted for his wit and charm, held a curule aedileship in 90.
His candidacy for the consulship without having been pra-

---

[44]Cic. *Att.* 4.8a.1–2: *Quid enim hoc miserius quam eum qui tot annos quot habet designatus consul fuerit fieri consulem non posse, praesertim aut solus aut certe non plus quam cum altero petat?*; Plut. *Pomp.* 51.4–52.1; *Crass.* 15.1–4; *Cat. Min.* 41–42; *Caes.* 21.3–4; App. *BC* 2.17; Dio 39.30–31; *MRR* 2.214–215.

etor is securely attested, and T. N. Mitchell (*CPh* 70 [1975] 197–204) has made a strong argument in favor of the view that he had secured from the Senate an exemption from the requirement to hold the praetorship first (Cic. *Phil.* 11.11; cf. *Har. Resp.* 43; Ascon. 25C). The precise date is disputed, whether he began late in 89 to compete for the consulship of 88 or, more probably, in 88 for that of 87; nor is the reason certain for Caesar's haste to attain the consulship. The summary account in Diodorus (37.2.12) has him aiming at the command against Mithridates, but it seems unlikely with Marius and Sulla on the scene. It is certain that the tribunes P. Antistius (18) and P. Sulpicius Rufus (92) opposed the candidacy from the start as illegal, first using legal methods (*iure*), a reference perhaps to the grant of exemption, and, when he continued, turned to force (Ascon. 25C; Cic. *Brut.* 226–227) and thus put an end to the candidacy.[45] The conflict with Caesar Strabo somehow led the tribune Sulpicius Rufus to leave his former optimate associations, turn to measures such as the return of the Varian exiles and the registration of the new Italian citizens and the freedmen in all the tribes, and the appointment of Marius to supplant Sulla in the command against Mithridates (*MRR* 2.41–42), which led swiftly to Sulla's march on Rome, and the death of Sulpicius himself. Caesar Strabo perished, along with his brother and many other leading men, in the Marian "massacre" when Marius and Cinna returned to power in Rome in the latter part of 87.

15. ? *T. Labienus* (6) Pr. by 59 ?

The position in 50 B.C. of T. Labienus, Caesar's legatus pro praetore since 58 in Gaul, is described as follows by Hirtius: *T. Labienum Galliae praefecit togatae, quo majore commendatione conciliaretur ad consulatus petitionem* (*BG* 8.52.2), this

---

[45]Ascon. 25C: *Gaius aedilicius quidem occisus est, sed tantum in civitate potuit ut causa belli civilis contentio eius cum Sulpicio tr. fuerit. Nam et sperabat et id egebat Caesar ut omissa praetura consul fieret; cui cum primis temporibus iure Sulpicius resisteret, postea nimia contentione ad ferrum et ad arma processit;* Cic. *Phil.* 11.11: *alter Caesar Vopiscus ille summo ingenio, summa potentia, qui ex aedilitate consulatum petit, solvatur legibus; Har. Resp.* 43: *Sulpicium ab optima causa profectum Gaioque Iulio consulatum contra leges petenti resistentem longius quam voluit popularis aura provexit;* Quintil. *Inst. Or.* 6.3.75; Macrob. *Sat.* 1.11.32.

For discussions of Strabo's candidacy, with the tribunate of Sulpicius and the complex issues of that time, see E. Badian, "Quaestiones Variae," *Historia* 18 (1969) 447–491, esp. 481–490; in favor of the earlier date, T. N. Mitchell, "The *Volte-Face* of P. Sulpicius Rufus in 88 B.C.," *CPh* 70 (1975) 197–104; A. W. Lintott, "The Tribunate of P. Sulpicius Rufus," *CQ* 21 (1971) 442–453; A. Keaveney, "Sulla, Sulpicius and Caesar Strabo," *Latomus* 38 (1979) 451–460; B. A. Marshall, *Asconius,* 144–146; and on the death of Caesar, Strabo, *ibid.,* 146.

although he had heard that his enemies in Rome had been in touch with him. This action, placing Labienus in charge of Cisalpine Gaul, could be regarded as a conciliatory gesture, but Syme accepts also the view that it was a preparation for Labienus to compete, probably with Caesar as his colleague, for the consulship of 48 (*Roman Papers* 1.62–75). The departure of Labienus early in January of 49 to join the forces opposed to Caesar ended any such plan. W. R. Tyrrell accepts Syme's interpretation of the passage, but while Syme attributes Labienus' action to his old and continued loyalty to Pompey, Tyrrell points to his contact with Caesar's enemies, the group about Cato, and suggests that his action represented a decision "to join a legitimate government in a struggle against a revolutionary proconsul who placed his dignitas above his country" (*Historia* 21 [1972] 424–440).

15a. *M. Lollius Palicanus* (21, cf. 8) Pr. by 59

Palicanus, as tribune of the plebs in 71, was active in securing the restoration in 70 of the powers of the tribunate (*MRR* 2.122). His candidacy for the consulship of 66 was cut short by the declaration of C. Calpurnius Piso, consul in 67, a conservative and a strong opponent of Palicanus, who was holding the election, that even if Palicanus should be elected he (Piso) would refuse to announce him.[46] Cicero's mention of Palicanus in *Att.* 1.1.1 may mean that, although he appeared to have no chance, he might have had some hope for 63, but there is no evidence of any action.

16. *Q. Lucretius Afella* (25)

Lucretius Afella was a leader in the Marian party who defected to Sulla (Vell. 2.27.6), under whose command he had charge of the siege of Praeneste (Liv. *Per.* 88; see *MRR* 2.72). When he insisted, against Sulla's order, on an illegal candidacy for the consulship, he was put to death at Sulla's command (Liv. *Per.* 89; Plut. *Sulla* 33.4; App. *BC* 1.101).[47]

---

[46]Val. Max. 3.8.3: *Deinde cum perseveranter instarent ac dicerent, "Age, si ventum fuerit?" "Non renuntiabo," inquit. Quo quidem tam absciso responso consulatum Palicano prius quam adipiscerentur eripuit;* cf. Vell. 2.92. On this passage, and on the legal force of the *renuntiatio,* see F. Cassola, *Gruppi politici Romani* 15; E. S. Staveley, *Greek and Roman Voting and Elections* 250–251, and note 206; R. Rilinger, *Einfluss* 145f.; Marshall, *Asconius* 220, 297, 301, and on 63, 281.

[47]G. V. Sumner (*Orators* 106–107), while noting that Appian states explicitly that Lucretius Afella was an *eques* and had held neither a quaestorship nor a praetorship, suggests that the words *Marianarum fuisset partium praetor* (Vell. 2.27.6) may mean that he had been a *praetor,* and his offence was that of becoming a consular candidate too soon

17. *T. Manlius Torquatus* (82) Cos. 235, 224, Cens. 231

In the election for the consulship of 210, when the *centuria praerogativa*, Voturia iuniorum, voted for the aged Manlius Torquatus, and for T. Otacilius Crassus (12), Manlius rejected candidacy because of age and failing strength, and bade the *centuria* to vote again. They consulted the corresponding *centuria* of seniors, and voted for M. Claudius Marcellus (220) and M. Valerius Laevinus (211) (Liv. 26.22.3–15; see *MRR* 1.277–278). Otacilius died near the end of the year (Liv. 26.23.8).

18. *L. Manlius Vulso* (92) Pr. 218 ?

Manlius Vulso was a candidate for the consulship of 216, who withdrew after the election of Terentius Varro (83) when L. Aemilius Paullus became a candidate (Liv. 22.34–35). See above, No. 1, on Q. Aelius Paetus (103).

19. *C. Memmius* (5) Pr. by 104

Memmius was a candidate in 100 for the consulship of 99, a competitor of C. Servilius Glaucia (65; see below, No. 25). In the election, after M. Antonius (28), the famous orator, had been elected, Memmius was murdered, during riots, by P. Mettius, an agent of Saturninus and Glaucia, who feared that his election would frustrate their plans.[48] On his praetorship, see *MRR* 1.559, 562, note 4; 3. 141; Sumner, *Orators*, 85–86.

20. *C. Memmius* (8) Pr. 58

Memmius, a candidate in 54 for the consulship of 53, became, like his competitors (see above, No. 4, on M. Aemilius Scaurus), deeply involved in massive bribery, and also, along with Cn. Domitius Calvinus (43), in a scandalous agreement with the consuls in office. His candidacy was delayed and weakened, and eventually he was prosecuted *de*

---

after it. E. Gabba suggested that since the period between Sulla's assumption of the dictatorship and the elections for 81 was so short, Afella was a candidate for the consulship of 80 or perhaps even of 79 (*Comm. on App. BC* 1, pp. 276–277). On the cognomen Afella, see Badian, *JRS* 57 (1967) 227–228.

[48]Liv. *Per.* 69: *Apuleius Saturninus trib. pleb. C. Memmium candidatum consulatus, quoniam adversarium eum actionibus suis timebat, occidit*; Oros. 5.17.5: *Saturninus Memmium, virum acrem et integrum, fieri consulem timens, orta subito seditione fugientem per P. Mettium satellitem informi stipite comminutum interfecit*; App. *BC* 1.32, and E. Gabba, *App. Bell. Civ. I*, pp. 110–112; cf. Cic. *Cat.* 4.4; Flor. 2.4.4; *MRR* 1.574–575, 575–576.

ambitu and convicted (Cic. *QF* 2.15.4, 16.2; 3.1.16; *Att.* 4.15.7, 17.2, 18.3; above, note 2). See Sumner, *HSPh* 86 (1982) 135–139; SB, *CLA* 1.331.

21. *T. Otacilius Crassus* (12) Pr. 212, 214

Otacilius received the vote of the *centuria praerogativa* in the elections for the consulship, both for 214 and for 210, but the *centuria* was persuaded to change its vote on both occasions (Liv. 24.7.10–9.6, and 26.22.15), and he was defeated. See above, No. 3, on M. Aemilius Regillus (138), and No. 17, on T. Manlius Torquatus (82).

22. *P. Plautius Hypsaeus* (23) Pr. by 55

Plautius was a candidate for the consulship of 52, competing with T. Annius Milo (67) and Q. Caecilius Metellus Scipio (99). See above, No. 5, on Milo. He had support from Clodius, then a candidate for the praetorship, whose followers after his murder brought the *fasces* from the grove of Libitina to the houses of both Hypsaeus and Metellus Scipio (Ascon. 33C). Although he had had some support from Pompey, under whom he had served as quaestor and proquaestor (Ascon. 35C, *MRR* 2.153, 164). Pompey rejected his appeal when he was prosecuted *de ambitu*, and he was convicted. See Ascon. 33–56C; Plut. *Pomp.* 55.6; Val. Max. 9.5.3; App. *BC* 2.24; Dio 40.53.1; and Marshall, *Asconius*, 160, 212.

23. *C. Scribonius Curio* (10) Pr. by 80

Curio was a candidate for the consulship of 77, but withdrew in favor of a competitor, Mam. Aemilius Lepidus Livianus (80), who had been defeated the previous year (Sall. *Hist.* I, fr. 86 M; see above, Part 1, No. 3, on Lepidus Livianus). Curio was elected consul for 76 (*MRR* 2.92).

24. *L. Sergius Catilina* (23) Pr. 68

Catiline made his first attempt to compete for the consulship immediately after his return from his praetorian province of Africa in 66. L. Volcatius Tullus, consul in charge of the elections for 65, after consultation with his *consilium*, refused to accept his candidacy, formally because Catiline was unable to make his *professio* the number of days required by law before the election.[49] See Part 1, No. 33, above on the candidacies for the consulships of 63 and 62.

25. *C. Servilius Glaucia* (65) Pr. 100

Servilius Glaucia, while still praetor in 100 and acting in alliance with the tribune L. Appuleius Saturninus (29), moved illegally to be a candidate for the consulship of 99, even though his *ratio* had not been accepted.[50] In the riotous election proceedings that followed he was a party to the murder of C. Memmius (5), a superior competitor.[51]

When Marius and his forces, acting under the *senatus consultum ultimum*, proceeded against Saturninus and Glaucia, they and their followers retired to the Capitolium,[52] where they were besieged and forced to surrender. Marius placed them in the Curia to await trial, but, although they had been given *publica fides*, they were attacked by an opposing mob and perished. Glaucia was killed when he was dragged from the house of a certain Claudius, to which he had somehow escaped (Oros. 5.17.4–10). See *MRR* 1.574–576; 3.20–22, on Saturninus.

---

[49]See R. Seager, "The First Catilinarian Conspiracy," *Historia* 23 (1964) 338–347, esp. 338–339; G. V. Sumner, "The Consular Elections of 66 B.C.," *Phoenix* 19 (1965) 226–231, with discussion of earlier and opposing views. Note Sall. *Cat.* 18.3: *Post paullo* (after the conviction of P. Sulla and Autronius) *Catilina pecuniarum repetundarum reus* (not until 65!) *prohibitus erat consulatum petere, quod inter legitimos dies profiteri nequiverat;* Ascon. 89C: L. *Volcatius Tullus consul consilium publicum habuit an rationem Catilinae habere deberet, si peteret consulatum: nam quaerebatur repentundarum. Catilina ob eam causam destitit a petitione.* As the trial of Catiline did not take place until 65 (Ascon. 85C), it could hardly have prevented his candidacy in 66, but did, of course, preclude it in 65. On the whole problem, see Marshall, *Asconius*, 302–305.

[50]Cic. *Brut.* 224: *Is ex summis et fortunae et vitae sordibus in praetura consul factus esset, si rationem eius habere licere iudicatum esset.*

[51]App. *BC* 1.32, and E. Gabba, App. *BC* 1, pp. 111–112; Vell. 2.12.6; Oros. 5.17.5. See above, No. 19, on C. Memmius (5).

[52]They probably retired for refuge, but perhaps, as Badian suggests (*Chiron* 14 [1984] 101–147, esp. 106), in an attempt to call an assembly and through it to get an exemption from the *Leges Annales* for Glaucia's candidacy; but note the phrase in the Elogium of Marius *qui armati Capitolium occupaverant* (Degrassi, *Inscr. Ital.* XIII, 3, *Elogia* 83).

III. CANDIDATES FOR THE CENSORSHIP

1. *M'. Acilius Glabrio* (35) Cos. 191

Acilius Glabrio, victor over Antiochus III at Thermopylae in 191, was a candidate for the censorship in 189, a *novus homo* against five distinguished competitors in a hotly contested election (Liv. 37.57.9–58.2). Three of them, T. Quinctius Flamininus (45), Cos. 198, P. Cornelius Scipio Nasica (350; see below, No. 4), L. Valerius Flaccus (173; see below, No. 15), were patricians, and the other three, M. Claudius Marcellus (222), Cos. 196, M. Porcius Cato (9), Cos. 195 (see below, No. 9), and Acilius himself were plebeians. All six were consulars. Acilius had celebrated a triumph, had won popular support by extensive largesse, and had Scipionic backing, but two tribunes, with Cato among the witnesses, indicted him for appropriation of booty from the camp of Antiochus which had not appeared in his triumph and had not been brought to the treasury, but pressed the charge no further when he withdrew. Livy ascribes the opposition to envy of a popular "new man." It may also be a sign of the weakening of Scipionic influence. T. Quinctius Flamininus and M. Claudius Marcellus were elected. See *MRR* 1.360–361; Suolahti, *RC* 340, 646.

2. *Ap. Claudius Pulcher* (295) Cos. 143.

Claudius Pulcher was a rival in 142 of Scipio Aemilianus in the election for the censorship for the patrician place and was defeated (Plut. *Aem.* 38.3–4; Cic. *Scaur.* 32). He was elected with Q. Fulvius Nobilior (95) to the censorship of 136 (*MRR* 1.486). See Suolahti, *RC* 383, 398–401.

3. *L. Cornelius Scipio Asiaticus* (337) Cos. 190

L. Scipio Asiaticus, brother of Africanus, was a candidate for the censorship in 184, at a time when Scipionic influence had been very seriously weakened by the attacks of the Elder Cato and "The Trials of the Scipios." His competitors were four patricians, P. Cornelius Scipio Nasica (350), his

31

cousin (see below, No. 4), making his second attempt, L. Furius Purpurio (86; see below, No. 6), Cn. Manlius Vulso (91; see below, No. 8), and L. Valerius Flaccus (173; see below, No. 15), also for the second time, and four plebeians, M. Fulvius Nobilior (91; see below, No. 5), Ti. Sempronius Longus (67; see below, No. 12), Ti. Sempronius Tuditanus (95; see below, No. 13), and the candidate who dominated both the hotly contested election and the subsequent censorship, M. Porcius Cato (9; see below, No. 10), in his second attempt. See Liv. 39.40.6–41.4, and 42.5–45.9; Plut. *Cat. Mai.* 16–19. L. Valerius Flaccus was elected with Cato (Liv. 39.41.4; Suolahti, *RC* 347–348; *MRR* 1.374–375. In their survey as censors of the Equites, they ordered Scipio Asiaticus to give up his horse (Liv. 39.44.1).

4. *P. Cornelius Scipio Nasica* (350) Cos. 191

Scipio Nasica was a candidate for the censorship of 189 (Liv. 37.57.9–58.2), and again for that of 184 (Liv. 39.40.1–41.4), and was defeated both times (cf. Suolahti, *RC* 258, 358). See above, No. 1, on Acilius Glabrio, and No. 3, on Scipio Asiaticus.

5. *M. Fulvius Nobilior* (91) Cos. 189

Fulvius Nobilior, a candidate for the censorship of 184, was defeated by the election of M. Porcius Cato and L. Valerius Flaccus (Liv. 39.40.6–41.4). See above, No. 3, on Scipio Asiaticus. In his second candidacy in 179 he was elected along with his enemy of long standing, M. Aemilius Lepidus (68). The stage was thus set for a resounding public reconciliation, which was often referred to as a model of laying down private quarrels for the public good (Liv. 40.45.6–46.16; Cic. *Prov. Cons.* 20). See Suolahti, *RC* 348, 361; *MRR* 1.392. On their enmity, see above, Chapter II, Part 1, No. 2, on M. Aemilius Lepidus.

6. *L. Furius Purpurio* (86) Cos. 196

Furius Purpurio, a candidate for the censorship in 184, was defeated by the election of M. Porcius Cato and L. Valerius Flaccus (Liv. 39.40.1–41.4; Suolahti, *RC* 348–349). See above, No. 3, on Scipio Asiaticus.

7. *M. Iunius Brutus* (48) Cos. 178

Iunius Brutus was a candidate for the censorship of 169, with five competitors, three of them patricians, C. Claudius

Pulcher (500), Cos. 177, L. Postumius Albinus (41; see below, No. 11), and C. Valerius Laevinus (208; see below, No.
16), and two plebeians, P. Mucius Scaevola (16; see below,
No. 9) and Ti. Sempronius Gracchus (53), Cos. 177 (Liv.
43.14.1). Claudius Pulcher and Sempronius Gracchus were
elected (Liv. 43.14.1). See Suolahti, *RC* 371; *MRR* 1.423–424.

8. *Cn. Manlius Vulso* (91) Cos. 189

   Manlius Vulso was a candidate for the consulship of 184,
and was defeated by the election of Cato and Valerius Flaccus (Liv. 39.40.1–41.4; Suolahti, *RC* 347–348; *MRR* 1.374).
See above, No. 3, on Scipio Asiaticus.

9. *P. Mucius Scaevola* (16) Cos. 175

   Scaevola was a candidate for the censorship of 169, and
was defeated by the election of C. Claudius and Ti. Sempronius Gracchus (Liv. 43.14.1; cf. Suolahti, *RC* 371; *MRR*
1.423–424). See above, No. 7, on M. Iunius Brutus.

10. *M. Porcius Cato* (9) Cos. 195

    Cato was a candidate for the censorship of 189, and was
defeated by the election of T. Quinctius Flamininus and M.
Claudius Marcellus (Liv. 37.57.9–58.1). See *MRR* 1.360–361,
and above, No. 1, on M. Acilius Glabrio. Cato was outstand-
ingly successful in 184, when he was elected with L. Valerius Flaccus. See Suolahti, *RC* 338–34; *MRR* 1.374–375; and
Briscoe, *Comm.* 2.390–392.

11. *L. Postumius Albinus* (41) Cos. 173

    A candidate for the censorship of 169, Postumius Albinus
was defeated by the election of C. Claudius Pulcher and Ti.
Sempronius Gracchus (Liv. 43.14.1). See Suolahti, *RC* 371;
MRR 1.423–424; and above, No. 7, on M. Iunius Brutus.

12. *Ti. Sempronius Longus* (67) Cos. 194

    Sempronius Longus was a candidate for the censorship of
184, and was defeated by the election of M. Porcius Cato
and L. Valerius Flaccus (Liv. 39.40.1–41.4). See Suolahti, *RC*
348; *MRR* 1.374–375; and above No. 3, on L. Cornelius
Scipio Asiaticus (337).

13. *Ti. Sempronius Tuditanus* (95) Cos. 185

A candidate for the censorship of 184, Sempronius Tuditanus was defeated by the election of M. Porcius Cato and L.
Valerius Flaccus (Liv. 39.40.1–41.4). See Suolahti, *RC* 348–
350; *MRR* 1.374–375; and above, No. 3, L. Cornelius Scipio
Asiaticus (337).

14. ? *Cn. Servilius Caepio* (46) Cos. 141

Noting that Servilius Caepio and Metellus Macedonicus
cooperated in their unsuccessful indictment of Q. Pompeius
upon his return from Spain in 139 (Cic. *Font.* 23; Val. Max.
8.5.1), and in suppressing a slave revolt in Minturnae and
Sinuessa in 133 (Oros. 5.9.4; Obseq. 27b), L. Heyne has suggested that a defeat of Caepio in the election for the censorship of 131, the first time both censors were plebeians, is
the reason why they were not censors together then (*Historia*
27 [1978] 234–235). In a period when patrician consulars
who competed usually attained the censorship promptly
(Suolahti, *RC* 373–374, 405–409), Servilius Caepio won his
in 125, sixteen years after his consulship (*MRR* 1.510). There
appears to be no direct evidence of candidacy or defeat in
131.

15. *L. Valerius Flaccus* (173) Cos. 195

A candidate for the censorship in 189, closely allied with
M. Porcius Cato, Valerius Flaccus and Cato were both defeated by the election of T. Quinctius Flamininus and M.
Claudius Marcellus (Liv. 37.57.9–58.2). See Briscoe, *Comm.*
2.390–392; Suolahti, *RC* 348–350; *MRR* 1.374–375; and
above, No. 1, on Acilius Glabrio.

16. *C. Valerius Laevinus* (208) Cos. Suff. 176

A candidate for the censorship in 169, Laevinus was defeated by the election of Claudius Pulcher and Ti. Sempronius Gracchus (Liv. 43.14.1). See Suolahti, *RC* 371; *MRR*
1.423–424; and above, No. 7, on M. Iunius Brutus.

IV. CANDIDATES FOR THE PRAETORSHIP

1. Candidates Defeated in Elections

1. *Q. Aelius Tubero* (155)

Aelius Tubero was a candidate for a praetorship, probably for 128 or 127, and was defeated because the voters resented his Stoic parsimony: he had provided cheap and inelegant furnishings in the arrangement of a *triclinium* at a public banquet in honor of his recently deceased uncle, Scipio Aemilianus.[1]

2. *C. Alfius Flavus* (7)

Alfius was an unsuccessful candidate for a praetorship in 56,[2] but appears in 54, issuing edicts and presiding over trials, perhaps as a praetor, although Cicero calls him a *quaesitor*.[3]

3. *L. Calpurnius Bestia* (25)

The candidacy for a praetorship in which L. Bestia received support from Caelius Rufus was probably the one that led to his indictment for *ambitus*. Cicero defended him and won an acquittal on February 11, 56.[4] In fact, he was

---

[1]Val. Max. 7.5.1: *Rogatus ut triclinium sterneret lectulos Punicanos pellibus haedinis stravit et pro argentis vasis Samia exposuit;* Cic. *Mur.* 75–76; *Huius* (Scipio) *in morte celebranda graviter tulit populus Romanus hanc perversam sapientiam Tuberonis, itaque homo integerrinus . . . his haedinis pelliculis praetura deiectus est;* see *MRR* 3.5.

[2]Cic. *Vat.* 38: *Ecquisnam tibi dixerit C. Caesarem nuper Aquileiae, cum de quibusdam esset mentio facta, dixisse C. Alfium praeteritum permoleste tulisse.*

[3]He issued edicts (Cic. *QF* 3.1.24), and presided over the trial of Gabinius *de maiestate* (Cic. *QF* 3.3.3), and that of Plancius *de sodaliciis* (Cic. *Planc.* 43 and 104, where he is addressed as "C. Flave.") See *MRR* 2.222, and 227, note 3.

[4]Cic. *Cael.* 26: (Caelium) *studuisse praeturae; QF* 2.3.6; *A. d. III Id. Feb. dixi pro Bestia de ambitu apud praetorem Cn. Domitium.* Contrary to the view held by Austin (*Comm. on Cic. Pro Cael.,* App. VI, 154–156; and by me in *MRR* 3.46), this Bestia should be distinguished from the homonymous tribune of 62 who was a supporter of Catiline and an opponent of Cicero (*MRR* 2.174). As Gruen has pointed out (*Athenaeum* 49 [1971] 67–69), Cicero in his attacks upon him would not have failed to refer to his Catilinarian past. See SB, *CLQF* 2.3.6 (p. 178); *Onomasticon* 29.

probably an unsuccessful candidate several times, as Cicero in 43 declares that he had defended Bestia six times, secured his acquittal in five of them, but failed in the sixth. Bestia had to go into exile, but regained his status later, probably from Caesar or from Antony, in whose following he was at the time of Cicero's sarcastic attack on him for aiming at the consulship while still only an *aedilicius*.[5]

4. *L. Cornelius Sulla (Felix)* (392)

Sulla was defeated in his first candidacy for a praetorship, and reportedly claimed that it was because he had omitted the aedileship, thus depriving the people of the beast hunts and the show of wild animals from Africa that his African connections would enable him to provide, and would have been expected of him as a public duty if he had been an aedile in charge of public games. Plutarch expresses doubt of this explanation, and notes that he was successful the next year (*Sulla* 5.2; cf. Val. Max. 7.5.5). The precise dates for his defeat, his election and his command in Cilicia are disputed, but 96, 95 and 94 seem probable.[6]

5. ? *C. Fannius* (9)

C. Fannius was one of the three tribunes in office in 59 who continued to oppose Caesar and his measures. Two of these, C. Ancharius (3) and Cn. Domitius Calvinus (43), had advanced to the praetorship in 56 (*MRR* 2.208). Cicero refers at the same time to the excellent prospects of Fannius,[7] but he is not named then or later as a candidate or an elected magistrate in office. His promagistracies in 49 suggest that he had already held a praetorship.[8]

---

[5]Cic. *Phil.* 11.11.: *Qui consulatum in Bruti locum* [in 41] *se petere profitetur . . . Quam absurdum autem, qui praetor fieri non potuerit, petere eum consulatum? Nisi forte damnationem pro praetura putat . . . At hic, me defendente, quinquiens absolutus est, sexta palma urbana etiam in gladiatore difficilis;* cf. *Phil.* 13.26, on Antony's imagined senate in his camp: *aedilicii, corycus laterum et vocis meae Bestia.*

[6]On this problem, see Badian, *Studies,* 157–158, in favor of 99, 98, and 97; Sumner, *Athenaeum* 56 (1978) 395–396, who suggests an immediate but unattested candidacy and election to the aedileship of 98, after which he went on to the praetorship of 95, and command in Cilicia in 94; and Sherwin-White (*CQ* 27 [1977] 173–183; *JRS* 67 [1977] 62–75, esp. 70–72), writing with emphasis on the situation in Asia Minor, finds 96, 95, and 94 the preferable series of dates. See also *MRR* 3.73–74.

[7]Cic. *Sest.* 113: *quod iudicium populi Romani in honoribus suis futurum sit, nemini dubium esse debet;* cf. *Vat.* 16: *tertium scis ex illo obsesso atque adflicto tribunatu consularem hominem esse adulescentem consecutum;* cf. Schol. Bob. 135, 146 St.

[8]Cic. *Att.* 7.15.2: *cum imperio in Siciliam praemittitur;* cf. 8.15.3; Joseph, *AJ* 14.230: τοῦ ἀντιστρατήγου in Asia. Sumner considers this insufficient evidence (*Orators,* 144–145), but Shackleton Bailey accepts it (*CLA* 1.402). See *MRR* 2.222, 262; 3.90.

6. *M. Favonius* (1)

Favonius was defeated in 51 when he was a candidate for a praetorship of 50,[9] but he must have been elected to one in 49, as he is termed a *praetorius* in 48 (Vell. 2.53.1).[10]

7. *M. Porcius Cato (Uticensis)* (16)

A candidate for a praetorship in 55, Cato persisted not only through the obstructive tactics of Pompey and Crassus late in 56 and the delay of the elections into 55 but also after they had been elected consuls in the *interregnum* and Pompey had charge of the elections. By means of bribery, violence, and obstruction (when the *centuria praerogativa* voted for Cato, Pompey, who was presiding, and himself an augur, heard thunder in a clear sky and dismissed the assembly), they secured the election of Vatinius and excluded Cato from that year.[11] Cato was elected, without apparent difficulty, to a praetorship of 54 (*MRR* 2.221–222).

2. Candidates Who Withdrew or Were Prevented from Competing

1. *P. Clodius Pulcher* (48)

Clodius, as he had been curule aedile in 56, was entitled under the *Leges Annales* to compete for the praetorship in 53. According to Cicero (*Mil.* 24), he made a beginning, but upon seeing that the long delay in that year would give only a few months in office, and wanting to avoid having L. Aemilius Paullus as a colleague, he deserted his own proper year and transferred his candidacy to 52, the next year, not, so Cicero states, because of any scruple, but, as he himself was saying, in order to have a whole year unimpaired for his praetorship.[12] His quarrels with Annius Milo,

---

[9]Caelius Rufus (35) in Cic. *Fam.* 8.9.5; *Nolo te putare Favonium a columniariis praeteritum; optimus quisque eum non facit.*

[10]Favonius was a constant associate and follower of Cato. See SB, *CLA 1.331; MRR* 3.90–91.

[11]See Cic. *QF* 2.8(7).3, and SB, *CLQF* p. 189; Dio 39.32.1–3; Cic. *Fam.* 1.9.19; Val. Max. 7.5.6; Liv. *Per.* 105; Plut. *Cat. Min.* 42, and *Pomp.* 52.1–2; cf. *MRR* 2.221–222, and 216 (on Vatinius). See R. Fehrle, *Cato Uticensis,* 166–174; Marshall, *Asconius,* 123.

[12]Cic. *Mil.* 24: *P. Clodius cum statuisset omni scelere in praetura vexare rem publicam videretque ita tracta esse comitia anno superiore, ut non multos menses praeturam gerere posset, qui non honoris gradum spectaret, ut ceteri, sed et L. Paulum collegam effugere vellet, singulari virtute civem, et annum integrum ad dilacerandam rem publicam quaereret, subito reliquit annum*

a candidate for a consulship in 52, and his own tumultuous candidacy prevented the holding of elections on into 52, and came to a sudden stop when he was killed by members of Milo's armed guard in a clash of their forces at Bovillae on January 18, 52 (Ascon. 30–32C; Cic. *Mil. passim*).

2. Q. Fulvius Flaccus (61)

Fulvius was a candidate for a suffect praetorship in 184, for the place of C. Decimus Flavus (8), praetor urbanus, who had died early in his year. His competitors were Cn. Sicinius (87) and L. Pupius (5), aediles of the plebs in 185, and C. Valerius Flaccus (166), Flamen Dialis (Liv. 39.39.2). Livy terms Fulvius *aedilis curulis designatus* at the time, but he must have been actually in office as 184 was a plebeian year (Mommsen, *StR* I³, 513, note 3). The objection to his candidacy was the possible cumulation of magistracies, which had been made illegal long before (Liv. 7.42.4, in 342). When Fulvius persisted with popular support, the consul, Porcius Licinus, and the Senate, in order to avoid any possibility of cumulation of magistracies, decreed that the praetor peregrinus, P. Cornelius Cethegus (75), should assume the duties of the deceased praetor urbanus, and that there should be no election for a suffect praetor that year (Liv. 39.39.1–5).[13] Fulvius was elected a praetor for 182, and consul for 179 (*MRR* 1.382, 391–392).

3. (C.?) Postumus (4) or C. Postumius (12)

Postumus is the name in the manuscripts of Cicero's *Pro Murena*, of a subscriptor in the indictment for *ambitus* brought by the defeated candidate, Ser. Sulpicius Rufus (95), against L. Licinius Murena, consul designate for 62, in the autumn of 63. This Postumus had been a candidate for a praetorship in that same year but had withdrawn.[14] There

---

suum seseque in proximum transtulit, non, ut fit, religione aliqua, sed ut haberet, quod ipse dicebat, ad praeturam gerendam, hoc est ad evertendam rem publicam, plenum annum atque integrum. Badian (*Studies*, 149–150) suggests that Cicero may have misinterpreted Clodius' decision, and that perhaps in fact 53 was the year for his *professio* for the praetorship of 52. See also Lintott, "Cicero and Milo," *JRS* 64 (1974) 66, and note 60; Marshall, *Asconius* 162.

[13]See A. E. Astin, "*Professio* in the Abortive Election of 184 B.C.," *Historia* 11 (1962) 252–256.

[14]Cic. *Mur.* 57: *Respondebo igitur Postumo primum qui nescio quo pacto mihi videtur praetorius candidatus in consularem quasi desultorius in quadrigarum curriculum incurrere. Cuius competitores si nihil deliquerunt, dignitati eorum concessit, cum petere destitit;* cf. 54, 56, 69.

has been much dispute as to whether his name was Postumus or Postumius.[15]

4. *L. Pupius* (3)

Pupius' candidacy for the suffect praetorship in 184 ended when the consul and the Senate decided not to hold an election (Liv. 39.39.1–15). See above, No. 2, on Q. Fulvius Flaccus (61). Pupius was elected a praetor for 183 (*MRR* 1.379).

5. *P. Sextius* (9)

Sextius was elected to a praetorship, but while *designatus* was indicted by a former tribune, T. Iunius L. f. (32), and convicted.[16] The date is uncertain, perhaps about 90 B.C.

6. *Cn. Sicinius* (8)

Sicinius' candidacy for a suffect praetorship in 184 ended with the decision of the consul and the Senate not to hold an election (Liv. 39.39.1–15). See above, No. 2, on Q. Fulvius Flaccus. Sicinius was elected to praetorships in 183 and 172 (*MRR* 1.378–379, 411 and 414, note 1).

7. *C. Valerius Flaccus* (166) Flamen Dialis

The candidacy of Valerius Flaccus for a suffect praetorship in 184 ended when the consul and the Senate decided not to hold an election (Liv. 39.39.1–15). See above No. 2, on Q. Fulvius Flaccus (61). In spite of being handicapped by the rules of his priesthood, Valerius competed successfully for a praetorship in 183 (*MRR* 1.378–79).

---

[15]In spite of the difficulty caused by emending Postumus in the text of the *Pro Murena* to Postumius in four passages out of five, Sumner and Shackleton Bailey agree, probably rightly, in making this change, but still disagree regarding the Postumii with which to identify him. See G. V. Sumner, *Phoenix* 25 (1971) 254, notes 26 and 27; *Orators* 144–145; *CPh* 73 (1978) 161; SB, *Two Studies* 58–60; cf. *Onomasticon* 80; and *MRR* 3.172.

[16]Cic. *Brut.* 180: *T. Iunius L. f. tribunicius, quo accusante P. Sextius praetor designatus damnatus est ambitus.* See G. V. Sumner, *Orators,* 108–109; *MRR* 3.111.

V. CANDIDATES FOR THE AEDILESHIPS

Candidates for either of the two aedileships, curule or plebeian, have been gathered here into a single list because it is not always certain for which one they were competing, but it is stated in each instance whenever it is known. The two aedileships were, of course, quite different in nature and origin, whatever resemblances may have developed in their duties. The plebeian aedileship was as old as the tribunate of the plebs, and could be held only by plebeians. They were elected in the *concilium plebis* with a tribune presiding. The curule aedileship was created in 367 at the time when the consulship was opened to plebeians. The first incumbents were patricians, were frequently already consulars, but very soon the magistracy began to be held by patricians and plebeians in alternate years. In the Late Republic they competed together. The curule aediles were elected in the *comitia tributa* with a consul or a praetor presiding. In the development of the *cursus honorum* this magistracy could be omitted, but if held it came before the praetorship and was subject to the intervals prescribed in the *Leges Annales*.

1. Candidates Defeated in Regular Elections

1. *Ap. Claudius Pulcher* (296) Cos. 79

   Ap. Claudius was defeated when a candidate for the curule aedileship (Cic. *Planc.* 51), probably in 95 or 94. He must have been successful soon afterward, as he had charge of the Ludi Megalenses (Cic. *Har. Resp.* 26), a duty incumbent on the curule aedile. The latest date is 92, as he held a praetorship in 89.[1]

2. *P. Cornelius Scipio (Nasica) Serapio* (354) Cos. 138
   or
   P. Cornelius Scipio (Nasica) Serapio (355) Cos. 111

   A Scipio Nasica, a candidate for the curule aedileship, while canvassing the voters, shook the hand of a rustic

---

[1]Cic. *Arch.* 9; cf. J. O. Lenaghan, *Comm. on Cic. Har. Resp.* 128–129; MRR 2.33.

voter with heavily calloused hands, and in jest asked him:
"Do you usually walk with your hands?" Members of the
rustic tribes took this to be an insult, and it lost him the
election.[2] Münzer was inclined to identify the Scipio named
in this anecdote with the consul of 138 (354), but admits that
he may be the consul of 111 (355), and would date the incident either to ca. 144 for the former or to ca. 118 for the
latter.

3. Cn. Domitius Calvinus Maximus (45) Cos. 283

Pliny, probably quoting from the *Annales* of L. Calpurnius
Piso Frugi (96), says that the election of Cn. Flavius (Cn. f.
or Anni f.) to a curule aedileship for 304, along with Anicius
Praenestinus (5), involved the defeat of two candidates, C.
Poetilius (2) and Domitius, both of them sons of consuls.[3]
Domitius may be tentatively identified as the consul of 283,
who is recorded from Piso by Livy (10.9.12–13) as curule
aedile in 299 (*MRR* 1.173). See below, No. 10, on C. Poetilius.

4. L. Iulius Caesar (142) Cos. 90

L. Caesar was defeated when a candidate for a curule
aedileship, probably ca. 99 B.C. since he held a praetorship
in 95 (*MRR* 2.11, and 14, note 3), a defeat of which Cicero
reminds Laterensis in *Pro Plancio* 51. See Shackleton Bailey,
Onomasticon 57.

5. M. Iuventius Laterensis (16) Pr. 51

Laterensis was a candidate, with A. Plautius (8) and Cn.
Plancius (4), for a curule aedileship of 55 or 54, more prob-

---

[2]Val. Max. 7.5.2: *Cum aedilitatem curulem adulescens peteret manuque cuiusdam rustici opere duratum more candidatorum tenacius adprehendisset, ioci gratia interrogavit eum num manibus solitus esset ambulare. Quod dictum a circumstantibus exceptum ad populum manavit causamque repulsae Scipioni attulit.* Valerius Maximus identifies him with the consul of 111, but this is vitiated by identification also with the Scipio Nasica who received the Mater Idaea in Rome.

In a passage in the *Pro Plancio* (51) Cicero is ostensibly attempting to remove any feel-ing of shame that Iuventius Laterensis might have after his defeat (see below, No. 5, Laterensis) when facing the *imagines* of his distinguished ancestors by reminding him of a series of such misfortunes suffered by distinguished men of an earlier generation which his grandfather could have witnessed and reported to him. The P. Nasica men-tioned there *(avus vero tuus et P. Nasicae tibi aediliciam praediceret repulsam)* was most prob-ably the consul of 138 (SB, *Onomasticon* 41), and the defeat perhaps the one mentioned above.

[3]Plin. *NH* 33.17: *libertino patre alioqui genitus et ipse scriba Appi Caeci . . . ut aedilis curulis crearetur cum Q. Anicio Praenestino qui paucis ante annis hostis fuisset, praeteritis C. Poetilio et Domitio, quorum patres consules fuerant;* cf. Peter, *HRR* 1.130–132, on L. Calpurnius Piso Frugi (96), frag. 27; Liv. 9.46.1; Val. Max. 2.5.2.

ably of 55,[4] who after his defeat prosecuted the successful
Plancius for bribery under Crassus' recent law *de sodaliciis*
(Cic. *Planc. passim*, esp. 49–50; cf. *QF* 3.1.11; Schol. Bob. 152
St). Cicero delivered the *Pro Plancio* in his defence and won
his acquittal.

6. C. Lucilius Hirrus (25)

Hirrus was a candidate, one of three, for a curule aedileship of 50, defeated by the election of M. Octavius (33) and
M. Caelius Rufus (55). See Caelius' letters to Cicero, *Fam.*
8.2.2, 3.1, 4.3, and 9.1; Cicero, *Fam.* 2.10.1, to Caelius.[5] See
Marshall, *Asconius* 76.

7. C. Marius (14, Supb. 6) Cos. 107, 104–100, 86

Marius was a candidate for the curule aedileship who,
when defeated, became at once a candidate for an aedileship of the plebs, and was defeated a second time.[6] The
year was probably 117, as he had been a tribune of the plebs
in 119 and held a praetorship in 115 (*MRR* 1.526, 532).

8. Cn. Octavius (20) Cos. 87

Octavius was a candidate for an aedileship whose defeat
Cicero lists with those of several others who later attained
the consulship (*Planc.* 51: *aedilitate praeteritos consules esse fac-
tos*), without specifying which of the individual examples refer to a curule or a plebeian aedileship. As Octavius held a
praetorship in 90, his candidacy for an aedileship may be
dated ca. 95 B.C. See SB, *Onomasticon* 72; Sumner, *Orators*
105, 115; *MRR* 2.26, 46; 3.151.

9. Q. Pedius (1) Pr. 48, Cos. Suff. 43

Pedius was a candidate for a curule aedileship, probably
of 55 (cf. above, No. 5, on Iuventius Laterensis, and note 4),
who is stated to have arranged, in the incomplete first elec-

---

[4]On the question whether the election was for the curule aedileship of 55 or of 54, see
L. R. Taylor, *Athenaeum* 42 (1964) 12–28; and J. Linderski, *Studi Volterra* 2.284–302; *MRR*
3.158, all in favor of 55; and Sumner, *Phoenix* 25 (1971) 249, in favor of 54.

[5]Caelius in Cic. *Fam.* 8.9.1: *"Sic tu,"* inquit, *"Hirrum tractasti?"* Immo, si scias quam facile,
quam ne contentionis quidem minimae fuerit, pudeat te ausum illum umquam esse incedere tam-
quam tuum competitorem. Post repulsam vero risus tacit. On Hirrus, see SB, CLF 1.386–387,
388; CLA 2.202; MRR 2.248–249; 3.129.

[6]Marius was one of Cicero's examples in *Planc.* 51: *qui duabus aedilitatis acceptis repulsis
septiens consul est factus;* cf. Plut. *Mar.* 5.1–2. See T. F. Carney, *A Biography of Marius* 21.

tion of the two for the position, with a competitor, A. Plotius, to receive through him the vote of the tribe Aniensis (Cic. *Planc.* 17.34). Pedius held a praetorship in 48, and was elected consul suffectus with Octavian on August 19, 43 (*MRR* 2.273, 336–337). He was a nephew of Julius Caesar and one of his heirs (Suet. *Caes.* 83.2).

10. C. Poetilius (2)

Poetilius was a candidate for a curule aedileship of 304, along with a Domitius, but both were defeated by the election of Cn. Flavius and Q. Anicius Praenestinus. See above, No. 3, on Cn. Domitius Calvinus (45).

11. M. Pupius Piso Frugi (Calpurnianus) (10) Cos. 61

Pupius Piso was a candidate for a curule aedileship who was defeated (Cic. *Planc.* 12, 51). The election was held in 75, as his competitor, M. Seius, was in office in 74 (*MRR* 2.102). He held a praetorship in 72 or 71 (*MRR* 2.117; 3.177), and was consul in 61 (*MRR* 2.178).

12. M. Tullius Decula (34) Cos. 81

The M. Tullius who was a candidate for an aedileship and was defeated (Cic. *Planc.* 51) may be identified with the consul of 81 (*MRR* 2.74). See SB, *Onomasticon*, 95. His praetorship must have preceded 84, but is not mentioned, nor is there evidence for the date of his candidacy for the aedileship.

13. P. Vatinius (3) Cos. 47

Vatinius was a candidate for an aedileship of 56, who was defeated when the election was finally held on January 20 of that year, even failing to win the vote of his own tribe.[7] With the support of Pompey and Crassus, he defeated Cato for a praetorship in 55 (*MRR* 2.216; see above, Praetors, Part 1, No. 7, on M. Porcius Cato), and received a consulship under Caesar in 47 (*MRR* 2.286).

---

[7]Cic. *Sest.* 114: *Alter* (Vatinius) . . . *aedilitatem petivit cum bonis viris et hominibus primis sed non praestantissimis opibus et gratia tribum suum* (Sergia, *Vat.* 36) *non tulit, Palatinum denique . . . perdidit, nec quicquam illis comitiis quod boni viri vellent nisi repulsam tulit;* cf. *Sest.* 135; *Vat.* 16, 31, and 38; *Har. Resp.* 56.

14. *L. Volcatius Tullus* (8) Cos. 66

Volcatius is described as a candidate for an aedileship who was defeated but later obtained the highest honors (Cic. *Planc.* 51: *summos honores*). There is no evidence regarding the date of his candidacy except that he must have been a praetor by or before 69 (*MRR* 2.132).

2. Candidates Who Withdrew or Remain Uncertain

1. *Ap. Claudius Pulcher* (297) Pr. 57, Cos. 54

Ap. Claudius was a candidate for the curule aedileship of 57 but then learned that by canceling his candidacy *(interversa aedilitate)* he could be elected, perhaps by fraud, to the praetorship of that same year. With the support of the consul, L. Calpurnius Piso (90), he withdrew immediately and stowed away the numerous objects in his possession which he had collected for display in the games of his aedileship.[8]

2. *? C. ? Claudius Marcellus* (216) Cos. 50

A certain Marcellus, a neighbor of Cicero on the Palatine, is named in a letter of Cicero,[9] written on November 3, 57, as a candidate, almost certainly for a curule aedileship of 56. There is no certain record of his defeat or his success when Clodius was finally elected about January 20, 56 (Cic. *QF* 2.3.1), but 56 is a probable year for a consul of 50, and prospects for a Claudius Marcellus were quite favorable. See also *MRR* 2.208; 3.54; SB, *CLA* 2.178.

---

[8]Cic. *Dom.* 112: *Is postea quam intellexit posse se interversa aedilitate a L. Pisone consule praetorem renuntiari, si modo eadem prima littera competitorem habuisset aliquem, aedilitatem duobus in locis, partim in arca, partim in hortis suis conlocavit.* See SB, *CLA* 1.396; 2.155.
[9]Cic. *Att.* 4.3.5: *Marcellus candidatus ita stertebat ut ego vicinus audirem.* Cf. *MRR* 2.208; SB, *CLA* 2.178.

VI. CANDIDATES FOR THE TRIBUNATE OF THE PLEBS

1. *Cn. Aufidius Orestes* (12) Cos. 71

Cn. Orestes, whom Cicero names as one who, though defeated when a candidate for the tribunate, later attained the consulship (*Planc.* 52), seems best identified with the consul of 71 named above (*MRR* 2.121). He was an Aurelius Orestes who was adopted by an Aufidius in his old age (Cic. *Dom.* 35; SB, *Two Studies* 84–85, 105; *Onomasticon* 21). The date of his defeat was probably before 82, as candidates with ambitions for a further career would have avoided the tribunate between 81 and 75.

2. *C. Cassius Longinus* (57) Cos. 96
or
C. Cassius Longinus (58) Cos. 73

The candidate for the tribunate, C. Cassius, whom Cicero mentions (*Planc.* 52), who was defeated but later attained the consulship, may be identified with the C. Cassius who was consul in 96 or the one who was consul in 73 (SB, *Onomasticon* 31), both active in the period from which Cicero drew his examples. If he was the former, the date may be about 105, but if the latter, before 82.

3. *? Flaminius* (7)

An obscure Flaminius is recorded by Appian (*BC* 3.31) as a candidate in the summer of 44 for a place in the college of tribunes of the plebs, perhaps the place made vacant by the death of C. Helvius Cinna (11, cf. 12; see *MRR* 2.324), and he had support from the young Octavian. As popular favor turned toward Octavian himself (App. *BC* 3.31) M. Antonius took measures to prevent an election. The identity of Flaminius remains obscure.

4. *C. Flavius Fimbria* (87) Cos. 104

The candidate, C. Fimbria, whom Cicero describes as one who, though defeated for the tribunate of the plebs, later attained the consulship (*Planc.* 52, cf. 12), seems best identified with the C. Flavius Fimbria who won the consulship as a colleague of Marius in 104 (*MRR* 1.558). See Wiseman, *New Men* 331, No. 180; SB, *Onomasticon* 49; and above, Chapter II, Part 1, No. 23, on Q. Lutatius Catulus.

5. *C. Marius* (14, Supb. 6) Cos. 107, 104–100, 86

C. Marius, whose career is described by Valerius Maximus (6.9.14) as *maximae fortunae luctatio*, is reported there to have been defeated when he was a candidate for the tribunate before he succeeded in winning it in 119. The report seems improbable as he had support at that time from the Metelli (Plut. *Mar.* 4.1), and there is no other mention of it. See T. F. Carney, *A Biography of Marius* 18; E. Gabba, "Marius and Sulla," *ANRW* 1.769–770; E. Badian, *DUJ* 25 (1963–64) 141–151; *MRR* 3.139–140.

6. ? *Sex. Nonius Sufenas* (53)

Plutarch (*Sulla* 10.2–4) mentions a Nonius, nephew of Sulla, who stood for some office (*arche*) in 88, when Sulla was consul, as a candidate he preferred, but was rejected by the people because the unpopularity of Sulla's actions. If, as seems probable, Nonius may be identified with Sextus Nonius Sufenas, known from the inscription on coins struck by M. Nonius Sufenas ca. 60 B.C. as the praetor in 81 who was the first to celebrate the *Ludi Victoriae Sullanae* (*MRR* 2.76, 447; 3.149; Crawford, *RRC* 1.no. 441, dated to 59; cf. Vell. 2.27.6), he was at that time probably competing for one of the lower offices. Drumann-Groebe (*RG*² II 559) suggests the tribunate of the plebs, but an aedileship or even a praetorship is not impossible. If Nonius was not Sex. Nonius Sufenas, there is no other information about him. See above, Chapter II, Part 1, No. 33a, on P. Servilius Vatia (Isauricus).

7. *A. Nunnius* (1)

A candidate for a tribunate of 99, Nunnius was, according to Appian (*BC* 1.28), a rival of Saturninus for the tenth place of the required ten. He was attacked and killed, according to Appian, when he had already been elected and was a tribune designate, but, according to Plutarch (*Mar.* 29.1),

Valerius Maximus (9.7.3), and Orosius (5.17.5), it was before he could be elected. See E. Gabba, *Appiani Bell. Civ. prim.*, pp. 101–102.

8. *P. Rutilius Rufus* (34) Cos. 105

Rutilius Rufus is named as a candidate for the tribunate of the plebs in Cicero's list of defeated tribunitial candidates who later attained the consulship (*Planc.* 52). As Rutilius held a praetorship by 118, his candidacy for the tribunate should be dated before 120 (*MRR* 1.527, 555).

VII. CANDIDATES FOR THE QUAESTORSHIP

1. ? *M. Favonius* (1) Pr. 49

In a letter written early in June of 60, Cicero comments on the defeat of Favonius by Nasica (Caecilius Metellus Scipio Nasica), and his unsuccessful prosecution of the victor, whom Cicero had defended, presumably on a charge *de ambitu*.[1] Since the date is too early in the year for any regular election, this election must have been intended to fill a vacancy, but there is disagreement as to whether the vacant place was that of an aedile, or a tribune of the plebs, or a quaestor. See SB, *CLA* 1.350–351; cf. *MRR* 3.41–42, a summary of opinions with some preference for a quaestorship.[2] According to Cicero, Favonius was standing for office again *rei publicae causa*, but there is no report of the results.

2. *Q. Lutatius Catulus* (7) Cos. 102
or

Q. Lutatius Catulus (8) Cos. 78

E. Badian's suggestion that the correct reading in Cicero, *Pro Plancio* 52, is not Q. (or C.) Caelius, but Q. Catulus (*Studies* 152–153) has been firmly accepted by Shackleton Bailey (*HSPh* 83 [1979] 277–278). The passage *(quaestor Q. Catulus)* records a defeat for a quaestorship, and may refer either to the consul of 102 or the consul of 78, perhaps preferably the former as more consistent with the dates of Cicero's other examples, and with a person well known for his series of defeats for the consulship. See above, Chapter II, Part 1, No. 23.

---

[1]Cic. *Att.* 2.1.9: *Favonium meam tribum tulit honestius quam suam, Luccei perdidit. Accusavit Nasicam inhoneste ac modeste tamen . . . mihi quod defendissem leviter suscensuit. Nunc tamen petit iterum rei publicae causa.*

[2]Note that Favonius is named as a tribune of the plebs by Themistius (*Orat.* 3.4.8; cf. E. Champlin, *CPh* 84 [1989] 92), and that he was an aedile in 53 or 52, and a praetor in 49 (*MRR* 2.257, and 277; 3.90–91). See also C. Alford, *CR* 41 (1927) 215–218.

VIII. CANDIDATE FOR THE MILITARY TRIBUNATE

1. *L. Marcius Philippus* (75) Cos. 91. Pr. by 96

The L. Philippus whose defeat in an election for the office of *tribunus militum* Cicero mentions in *Pro Plancio* 52 should be identified with L. Marcius Philippus (75), consul in 91 (Shackleton Bailey, *Onomasticon* 66–67). The date may be ca. 106 B.C. See above, Chapter II, Part 1, No. 27, on this Marcius Philippus.

IX. CANDIDATES FOR THE PRIESTLY COLLEGES AND FOR PONTIFEX MAXIMUS

From early times the members of the major priestly colleges coopted in each college new members individually as an appointment for life to the places vacated by deceased members. But in 104 or 103 Cn. Domitius Ahenobarbus (21), in anger at not being coopted by the college of pontifices to the place vacated by the death of his father, carried a law while tribune of the plebs making membership in the major colleges subject to popular election by an assembly of seventeen tribes chosen by lot, one less than majority of the total of thirty-five tribes.[1] This law remained in force until 82 or 81, when Sulla restored the former practice, but in 63 a law carried by T. Labienus, when tribune of the plebs, made popular election by seventeen tribes a requirement again.[2] The former requirements of a formal recommendation by two members of the college and acceptance by a vote of the college also remained in use. Elections to the priestly colleges were regularly held in the interval between those for consuls and those of praetors, with a consul as presiding officer. From early times the pontifex maximus was elected by the assembly of seventeen tribes.[3] The candidate had to be a pontifex in office, with the most recently elected pontifex as the presiding officer.

1. *? M. Antonius* (30) Cos. 44, 34

A phrase in a letter of M. Antonius to Cicero shortly before the latter left Italy to join Pompey (*Att.* 10.8a.1, May 1, 49; cf. SB, *CLS* 4.410–411) which refers to some coolness or jealousy (ζηλοτυπία) between them has been taken as a reference to supposed jealousy on the part of Antonius when

---

[1] See *MRR* 1.559–560, 562, note 8; cf. 3.82–83, and also 10–12, on M. Aemilius Scaurus (140).

[2] See *MRR* 2.75, on Sulla, and 167–168, on Labienus.

[3] See L. R. Taylor, "The Election of the Pontifex Maximus in the Late Republic," *CPh* 37 (1942) 421–424. On the presiding officer, see Liv. 25.5.2; Mommsen, *StR* II³, 27, note 3. On the process of election, see J. Linderski, *HSPh* 76 (1972) 181–200, esp. 190–193.

Cicero was elected an augur, by 52 or, probably, in 53.[4] Whatever the reference may mean, Antonius did not compete at the time when Cicero was elected (Cic. *Phil.* 2.4), but did so successfully in 50. See below, No. 2, on L. Domitius Ahenobarbus (27).

2. *L. Domitius Ahenobarbus* (27) Cos. 54

A candidate for an augurate in 50 for the plebeian place made vacant by the death of Hortensius in June of that year (Caelius in Cic. *Fam.* 8.13.2; cf. SB, *CLF* 1.426), Domitius was defeated by the young M. Antonius, then a tribune designate, who had in his favor the support of Caesar and the memory of his grandfather, the famous orator, M. Antonius (28), Cos. 99.[5]

3. *L. Cornelius Lentulus Crus* (218) Cos. 49

A candidate in 51 for a place in the *Quindecimviri sacris faciundis*, Lentulus Crus was defeated by the young P. Cornelius Dolabella (141), the future consul suffectus of 44 (Caelius in Cic. *Fam.* 8.4.1: *caruisse te pulcherrimo spectaculo et Lentuli Cruris repulsi vultum non vidisse*; cf. SB, *CLF* 1.390).

4. *Q. Fulvius Flaccus* (59) Cos. 237, 224, 209

A candidate in 212 for election as pontifex maximus in succession to the deceased L. Cornelius Lentulus Caudinus (211), Cos. 237, Fulvius Flaccus was surprisingly defeated by the much younger P. Licinius Crassus (69), then a candidate

---

[4]See *MRR* 2.233; 3.209. Shackleton Bailey, "Notes on Cicero's Philippics," *Philologus* 126 (1982) 217–226, esp. p. 219, finds indications in Cicero's letters to Curio (*Fam.* 2.1–6, esp. 4–6) that Curio probably returned from Asia to Rome by late in 53. As Cicero was elected an augur before Curio's return (*Phil.* 2.4), he was very probably elected in 53. See in favor of election in 52, J. Linderski, *HSPh* 76 (1972) 187–200. See below, No. 5, on his competitor, C. Lucilius Hirrus (25).

[5]Caelius in Cic. *Fam.* 8.14.1: *numquam tibi oculi doluissent, si in repulsa Domiti vultum vidisses*, and SB, *CLF* 1.429–430. Hirtius in Caes. *BG* 8.50.1–3; cf. *Phil* 2.4, 78–84; Schol. Bern on Lucan 2.121, p. 57U; *MRR* 3.83–83. In the lacuna in Cic. *Fam.* 8.14.1: *quod per iniuriam sibi . . . ereptum*, Shackleton Bailey (*ICS* 2 [1977] 223–228; *CLF* 1.429–431) would supply the word *pontificatum* instead of the usual *auguratum*. This change means that Domitius, instead of trying to win the two major priesthoods, a very rare achievement, had failed earlier to win a place as pontifex, and was now doubly exasperated at failing, partly through Caelius' aid to Antonius, to win one as augur. He became a pontifex very soon as he was one at his death in 48, the place to which C. Octavius, the future Augustus, succeeded, probably in the autumn of 47 (*MRR* 2.284, 292; 3.83–84).

for the curule aedileship (Liv. 25.5.1–4; *MRR* 1.271).[6] See below, No. 7, on his rival, T. Manlius Torquatus (82).

5. *C. Lucilius Hirrus* (25) Tr. pl. 53

Lucilius Hirrus was a candidate in 52 or, more probably, in 53 for a plebeian place in the college of augurs as successor to P. Licinius Crassus (83), who had perished in the campaign against the Parthians at Carrhae, and was defeated by Cicero (Caelius in Cic. *Fam.* 8.3.1: *auguratus tuum competitorem*; 8.9.1; 2.15.1; cf. SB, *CLF* 1.388.394; *MRR* 2.228–9). On the date, see above, note 4.

6. *Q. Lutatius Catulus* (8) Cos. 78

Catulus was a candidate in 63 for election as pontifex maximus in succession to the recently deceased Q. Caecilius Metellus Pius (98), and was defeated by C. Iulius Caesar (131), the future dictator, who in 63 was a successful candidate for a praetorship (Sall. *Cat.* 49.1–2; cf. Suet. *Caes.* 13; Plut. *Caes.* 7.1–2; see *MRR* 2.172, notes 1 and 2).

7. *T. Manlius Torquatus* (82) Cos. 235, 224; Cens. 223

Manlius was a candidate in 212 for election as pontifex maximus in succession to L. Cornelius Lentulus Caudinus (213), and, like Q. Fulvius Flaccus (see above, No. 4), was surprisingly defeated by the young P. Licinius Crassus (69), then a candidate for a curule aedileship (Liv. 25.5.1–4). See *MRR* 1.271.

8. *P. Servilius Vatia Isauricus* (93) Cos. 79

A candidate in 63 for election as pontifex maximus in succession to the deceased Q. Caecilius Metellus Pius (98), the elder Servilius Isauricus was defeated, along with Q. Lutatius Catulus (8; see above, No. 6), by C. Iulius Caesar (131), the future dictator, who was elected in that year to a praetorship for 62 (Plut. *Caes.* 7.1–3; cf. Sall. *Cat.* 49.1; Suet. *Caes.* 13). See *MRR* 2.171, 172, notes 1 and 3.

9. *P. Vatinius* (3) Cos. 47

---

[6]In 120 years this honor had come only once to a candidate who had not held curule office (Liv. 25.3.4). See *MRR* 1.271.

In a letter to Atticus[7] in mid-April, 59, Cicero mentions the possibility that Vatinius, then a tribune of the plebs actively supporting Caesar, might even be made an augur, and in 56 in the *In Vatinium* attacks him scathingly for even conceiving the desire to become one in the place of Q. Caecilius Metellus Celer (86), consul in 60, who had died early in 59. There is no further mention of this or of an election. Vatinius attained the consulship under Caesar in 47, and probably became an augur at about the same time (in September, when Caesar returned to Italy from the East) as he states in a letter to Cicero from his command at Narona in Dalmatia in January of 44 that he had succeeded to the place of Ap. Claudius Pulcher, who had died in 48.[8]

[7]Cic. *Att.* 2.9.2 (April 16 or 17, 59): *Proinde isti licet faciant quos volunt consules, tribunos pl., denique etiam Vatini strumam sacerdoti διβάφῳ vestiant* (cf. SB, *CLA* 1.372); *Vat.* 19: *cogitarisne illo tuo intolerabili non regno—nam cupis id audire—sed latrocinio augur fieri in Q. Metelli locum.*

[8]Cic. *Fam.* 5.10a.2: *Si me Hercules Appi os haberem, in cuius locum suffectus sum, tamen hoc sustinere non possem.* See SB, *CLF* 1.428; *MRR* 2.204 and 293.

APPENDIX

In addition to the two groups described above under the names of the magistracies, those who were defeated in regular elections, and those who withdrew or were prevented from competing, there are a few examples of candidates who were successful in the elections but were afterward prevented from taking office because they were accused and convicted of election bribery *(ambitus)*. The consular elections for 65 provide two outstanding examples, P. Cornelius Sulla (386) and P. Autronius Paetus, (7), who won the election (Sulla *omnibus centuriis;* Cic. *Sulla* 91), and defeated L. Aurelius Cotta (102) and L. Manlius Torquatus (79). They were accused of *ambitus* and convicted, Sulla by the younger Manlius, son of the candidate, and Autronius by Cotta himself, and under the terms of the law carried by C. Calpurnius Piso in 67, lost both office and the right to compete later. See above, Chapter II, Part 1, No. 6, on Cotta, and No. 24, on Manlius. There were many such trials in the Late Republic, but apparently few convictions.

The misspelled name Hotensio at 108 B.C. in the Chronographer of 354 and the letters MN, da]MN[(atus) at the same date in a fragment of the *Fasti Capitolini* with the cognomen Scaurus on the next line, confirmed by the name M. AURELI SCA in the *Fasti Antiates Maiores* at 108, combine to indicate another case of success, trial and conviction, this time of a Hortensius (A. Degrassi, *Inscr. Ital.* XIII, Fasc. 1, pp. 54–55, 162–163, 476).

At the tribunicial level, the case of Servaeus (3) presents another example. He was successful in 51 in the elections for tribunes of 50, but accusation of *ambitus* and conviction while he was still *designatus* made his place available for C. Scribonius Curio (11) to win in the supplementary election (Cic. *Fam.* 8.4.2: *Servaeum designatum tribunum pr. condemnatum; cuius <in> locum C. Curio petiit.* [August 1, 51]; 8.5.3: *hos si<c> praeterito anno, Curio tribunus e<ri>t,* [mid-September 51]). See SB, *CLF* 1.390 and 397.

BIBLIOGRAPHY

Alexander, Michael C., "Praemia in the *Quaestiones* of the Late Republic," *CPh* 80 (1985): 20–32.

Alford, C., "Notes on Cicero's Letters to Atticus, Book II," *CR* 41 (1927): 215–218.

Astin, A. E., *The Lex Annalis before Sulla.* Collection Latomus 32. Brussels, 1958.
    Scipio Aemilianus. Oxford, 1976.
    Cato the Censor. Oxford, 1978.
    "Professio in the Abortive Election of 184 B.C.," *Historia* 11 (1962): 252–255.

Badian, E., *Studies in Greek and Roman History.* Oxford, 1964.
    "Marius and the Nobles," *DUJ* 25 (1963–1964): 141–154.
    "Q. Mucius Scaevola and the Province of Asia," *Athenaeum* 34 (1956): 104–123.
    "Quaestiones Variae," *Historia* 18 (1969): 447–491.
    "Tiberius Gracchus and the Beginning of the Roman Revolution," *ANRW* I (1972): 668–731.
    "The Death of Saturninus," *Chiron* 14 (1984): 101–147.

Bailey, D. R. Shackleton, *Cicero's Letters to Atticus.* 7 volumes. Cambridge, 1965–1970.
    Cicero: Epistulae ad Familiares. 2 volumes. Cambridge, 1977.
    Cicero: Epistulae ad Quintum Fratrem et ad M. Brutum. Cambridge, 1980.
    Cicero, *Philippics.* Edited and Translated. Chapel Hill and London, 1986.
    Two Studies in Roman Nomenclature. American Classical Studies 3. Atlanta, Ga., 1976.
    Onomasticon to Cicero's Speeches. Norman, Oklahoma, and London, 1988.
    "The Prosecution of Roman Magistrates-Elect," *Phoenix* 24 (1970): 162–168.
    "The Grievance of L. Domitius Ahenobarbus," *ICS* 2 (1977): 223–228.
    "On Cicero's Speeches," *HSPh* 23 (1979): 237–286.
    "Notes on Cicero's Philippics," *Philologus* 126 (1982): 217–226.

Balsdon, J. P. V. D., "Q. Mucius Scaevola and *ornatio provinciae*," *CR* 51 (1937): 8–10.

Bates, R. L., "*Rex in Senatu*. A Historical Biography of M. Aemilius Scaurus," *Proc. Am. Philos. Soc.* 130 (1986): 251–288.

Bloch, G. M., "M. Aemilius Scaurus: Étude sur l'histoire des parties au VIIe siècle de Rome," *Mélanges d'histoire ancienne. Bibliothèque de la Faculté de Lettres de Paris*, Vol. 25, 1–80. Paris, 1909.

Briscoe, J., *A Commentary on Livy, Books xxxi–xxxiii*. Oxford, 1973.
   A Commentary on Livy, Books xxxiv–xxxvii. Oxford, 1981.

Broughton, T. R. S., *The Magistrates of the Roman Republic*. Volumes 1–2, 1951–1952; Volume 3, 1986. Atlanta, Ga.

Brunt, P. A., "Three Passages from Asconius," *CR* n.s. 7 (1957): 193–195.

Carney, T. F., *A Biography of Marius 2*. Argonaut, Chicago, 1970.

Cassola, F., *I Gruppi Politici Romani nel III Secolo a. C.* Rome, 1963.

Chapman, C. M., "Cicero and P. Sulpicius Rufus (Tr. Pl. 88 B.C.)," *A Class* 22 (1979): 61–72.

Courtney, E., "The Prosecution of Scaurus in 54 B.C.," *Philologus* 105 (1961): 151–156.

Criniti, N., M. Aemilius Q. f. M. n. Lepidus. *"Ut ignis in stipula,"* *MIL* 30 (1969), Fasc. 4, 318–459.

Denniston, J. D., *M. Tulli Ciceronis in M. Antonium Orationes Philippicae Prima et Secunda, with Introduction, Notes and Appendices*. Oxford, 1926.

Develin, R., "Scipio Africanus and the Consular Elections of 148 B.C.," *Latomus* 37 (1978): 484–488.
   "Patrician Censors," *Antichthon* 14 (1981): 84–87.

Dorey, T. A., "The Elections of 216 B.C.," *RhM* 102 (1959): 249–252.

Evans, Richard J., "Missing Consuls, 104–100 B.C. A Study in Prosopography," *LCM* 10 (1985): 76–77.
   "Metellus Numidicus and the Elections for 100 B.C.," *AClass* 30 (1987): 65–68.

Fehrle, R., *Cato Uticensis*. Darmstadt, 1983.

Gabba, E., *Appiani Bellorum Civilium Liber Primus* (and commentary). Florence, 1958.

Gray, E. W., "The Consular Elections Held in 65 B.C.," *Antichthon* 13 (1979): 56–65, and Appendix, 65–67.

Gruen, E. S., *Roman Politics and the Criminal Courts, 149–78 B.C.* Cambridge, Mass., 1968.
    The Last Generation of the Roman Republic. Berkeley and Los Angeles, 1974.
    "The Lex Varia," *JRS* 55 (1965): 59–73.
    "Notes on the First Catilinarian Conspiracy," *CPh* 64 (1969): 20–24.
    "The Consular Elections for 53 B.C.," *Hommages à Marcel Renard*, (1969), 2.311–321.
    "Criminal Trials of the Late Republic: Political and Prosopographical Problems," *Athenaeum* 49 (1971): 54–69.
    "The Consular Elections for 216 B.C. and the Veracity of Livy," *CSCA* 11 (1978): 61–74.

Grummel, W. C., "The Consular Elections of 59 B.C.," *CJ* 49 (1953–1954): 351–355.

Hardy, E. G., "The Catilinarian Conspiracy in its Context: A Restudy of the Evidence," *JRS* 7 (1917): 153–228.

Henderson, Ch., Jr., "The Career of the Younger Aemilius Scaurus," *CJ* 53 (1957–1958): 194–206.

Heyne, L., "The Censorship of 131," *Historia* 27 (1978): 234–235.

Jahn, J., *Interregnum und Wahldictatur.* Frankfurt Althist. Stud. 3. Kallmunz, 1970.

Katz, B. R., "Caesar Strabo's Struggle for the Consulship,—and More," *RhM* 120 (1977): 45–63.

Keaveney, A., "Sulla, Sulpicius and Caesar Strabo," *Latomus* 38 (1979): 451–460.
    "Deux dates contestées dans la carrière de Sulla," *LEC* 48 (1980): 149–159.

Kienast, D., *Cato der Censor; seine Persöhnlichkeit und seine Zeit.* Heidelberg, 1954.

Kunkel, W. *Herkunft und sociale Stellung der römischen Juristen.* Graz-Wien Vienna Cologne, 1967.

Lenaghan, J. O., *A Commentary on Cicero's Oration De Haruspicum Responso.* The Hague, 1969.

Levick, B., "Sulla's March on Rome in 88 B.C.," *Historia* 31 (1982): 503–508.

Linderski, J., "Three Trials in 54 B.C.: Sufenas, Cato, Procilius, and Cicero, ad Atticum 4.15.4," *Studi E. Volterra* (Milano, 1971) 2.281–302.
"The Aedileship of Favonius, Cato the Younger, and Cicero's Election to the Augurate," *HSPh* 76 (1972): 151–200.
"Buying the Vote: Electoral Corruption in the Late Republic," *Anc. World* 11 (1985): 87–94.
"The Augural Law," *ANRW* II.16 (1986): 2145–2312.

Lintott, A. W., *Violence in Republican Rome.* Oxford, 1968.
"The Tribunate of P. Sulpicius Rufus," *CQ* 21 (1971): 442–453.
"Cicero and Milo," *JRS* 64 (1974): 62–78.

Luce, T. J., "Marius and the Mithridatic Command," *Historia* 19 (1970): 161–194.

McDermott, W. C., "De Lucceiis," *Hermes* 97 (1969): 213–246.

Malcovati, E., *Oratorum Romanorum Fragmenta Liberae Rei Publicae*². Turin, 1955.

Marshall, B. A., *Crassus, A Political Biography.* Amsterdam, 1976.
A Historical Commentary on Asconius. Columbia, Mo., 1985.
"Catilina, Court Cases and Consular Candidature," *SCI* 3 (1966–67): 127–37.
"Cicero and Sallust on Crassus and Catiline," *Latomus* 53 (1974): 804–813.
"The Date of Mucius Scaevola's Governorship of Asia," *Athenaeum* 54 (1976): 117–130.
"Two Court Cases in the Later Second Century B.C.," *AJPh* 98 (1977): 417–423.
"The Vote of a Body-Guard for the Consuls of 65," *CPh* 72 (1977): 318–340.

Marshall, B. A. and Baker, R. J., "The Aspirations of Quintus Arrius," *Historia* 24 (1975): 220–231.

Marshall, B. A. and Stanton, G. R., "The Coalition between Pompeius and Crassus," *Historia* 24 (1975): 205–219.

Mello, M., "Sallustio e le Elezioni Consulari di 66 a.C.," PP 18 (1963): 36–54.

Michels, A. K., *The Calendar of the Roman Republic.* Princeton, N. J., 1967.

Mitchell, T. N., "The *Volte-Face* of P. Sulpicius Rufus in 88 B.C.," *CPh* 70 (1975): 197–204.

Münzer, Fr., *Römische Adelsparteien und Adelsfamilien*[2]. Stuttgart, 1963.

Mommsen, Th., *Römisches Staatsrecht*. Leipzig, 1888.

Phillips, E. J., "Asconius' *Magni Homines*," *RhM* 116 (1973): 353–357.
   "Catiline's Conspiracy," *Historia* 25 (1976): 441–448.

Ramsey, J. T., "Cicero, *Pro* Sulla 68 and Catiline's Conspiracy in 66 B.C.," *HSPh* 86 (1982): 121–132.

Rilinger, R., *Der Einfluss des Wahlleiters bei den römischen Konsulwahlen von 366 bis 50 v. Chr.* Vestigia 24. Munich, 1976.

Ruebel, J. S., "The Trial of Milo in 52 B.C.: a Chronological Study," *TAPhA* 109 (1979): 231–249.

Sanctis, G. de, *Storia dei Romani*, III.2. Turin, 1916 (2nd ed. 1968).

Schur, W., "Das sechste Consulat des Marius," *Klio* 31 (1938): 313–322.

Seager, R., "The First Catilinarian Conspiracy," *Historia* 13 (1964): 338–347.
   "The Date of Saturninus' Murder," *CR* 17 (1967): 240–245.
   "Iusta Catilinae," *Historia* 22 (1973): 240–248.

Shatzman, I., "Scaurus, Marius and the Metelli: a Prosopographical Factional Case," *Anc. Soc.* 5 (1974): 197–222.

Sherwin-White, A. N., "Violence in Roman Politics," *JRS* 46 (1956): 1–9.
   "Ariobarzanes, Mithridates and Sulla," *CQ* 27 (1977): 173–183.

Staveley, E. C., "The Conduct of Elections during an Interregnum," *Historia* 3 (1954): 193–211.
   Greek and Roman Voting and Elections. London, 1972.

Sumner, G. V., *The Orators in Cicero's Brutus: Prosopography and Chronology*. Phoenix, Supplement 11. Toronto, 1973.
   "Manius or Mamercus ?," *JRS* 54 (1964): 41–48.
   "The Consular Elections of 66 B.C.," *Phoenix* 19 (1965): 226–231.
   "Elections at Rome in 217 B.C.," *Phoenix* 29 (1975): 250–259.
   "Sulla's Career in the Nineties B.C.," *Athenaeum* 36 (1978): 395–396.
   "The Coitio of 54 B.C. or Waiting for Caesar," *HSPh* 86 (1982): 133–140.

Suolahti, Jaakko, *The Roman Censors. A Study in Social Structure*. Helsinki, 1963.

Syme, Sir Ronald, "The Allegiance of Labienus," *JRS* 28 (1938): 113–125—Roman Papers I, 62–75 (1979).

Taylor, L. R., *Party Politics in the Age of Caesar.* Sather Classical Lectures 22. Berkeley, 1949.
   Roman Voting Assemblies from the Hannibalic War to the Dictatorship of Caesar. Jerome Lectures 8. Ann Arbor, 1966.
   "The Election of the Pontifex Maximus in the Late Republic," *CPh* 37 (1942): 421–424.
   "Magistrates of 55 B.C. in Cicero's Pro Plancio and Catullus 52," *Athenaeum* (Studi in Onore di E. Malcovati) 42 (1964): 12–28.
   "The Office of Nasica in Cicero, *Ad Atticum* 2.1.9," *Studies in Honor of B. L. Ullman* (Chapel Hill, 1964) 1.79–85.

Twyman, B. L., "Consular Elections for 216 B.C. and the *Lex Maenia de patrum auctoritate*," *CPh* 79 (1984): 285–294.

Tyrrell, W. S., "Labienus' Departure from Caesar in January of 49 B.C.," *Historia* 21 (1972): 424–440.

Ward, A. M., *Marcus Crassus and the Late Roman Republic.* Columbia, Mo., and London, 1977.

Weinrib, E. J., "The Prosecution of Roman Magistrates," *Phoenix* 22 (1968): 32–56.
   "The Prosecution of Magistrates-Designate," *Phoenix* 25 (1971): 145–150.

Wiseman, T. P., *New Men in the Roman Senate from 139 B.C.–A.D. 14.* Oxford, 1971.
   "Lucius Memmius and his Family," *CQ* 17 (1967): 297–302.

Yavetz, Z., "The Failure of the Catilinarian Conspiracy," *Historia* 12 (1963): 485–399.

INDEX OF DEFEATED CANDIDATES

The names of the candidates are listed below in groups, arranged, as in the text, according to the magistracies for which they were competing, or expected to compete, and within each group alphabetically by the names of their *gentes*, e.g., Acilia, Aemilia, etc. Individual candidates are identified by the number (in brackets) under which they are listed in their respective *gentes* in Pauly-Wissowa, *Realencyclopädie*. In each of the discussions of individual candidates there is given, when they are known, both the names of their defeated rivals, with cross-references to the separate discussions of each of them, and the names of the victors in each election.

CANDIDATES FOR THE CONSULSHIP
1. Candidates Defeated in Regular Elections

2. Candidates who withdrew or were prevented from competing

CANDIDATES FOR THE CENSORSHIP

CANDIDATES FOR THE PRAETORSHIP
1. Candidates Defeated in Elections

CANDIDATES FOR THE PRIESTLY COLLEGES

CANDIDATES FOR PONTIFEX MAXIMUS

APPENDIX: CANDIDATES ELECTED BUT CONVICTED FOR *AMBITUS*

1. Candidates for the Consulship:

2. Candidate for the Tribunate of the Plebs: